This book belongs to:

_____

The Existential Capitalist
Copyright © 2026 David Gloag
All rights reserved.

No part of this book may be reproduced in any form or transmitted by electronic or mechanical means, including information storage and retrieval systems, without written permission from the author, except with reasonable use in commentary or critical reviews.

[1] King James Bible, 1611. Public domain.

[2] The New King James Version®,
Copyright © 1984 Thomas Nelson, Inc.
Used with permission. All rights reserved.

[3] Holy Bible, New International Version®, NIV®
Copyright © 2011 Biblica, Inc.®
Used with permission. All rights reserved.

[4] The Saint Athanasius Academy Septuagint™,
Copyright © 2008 St. Athanasius Academy of Orthodox Theology
Used with permission. All rights reserved.

[5] World English Bible®. Public domain.

First edition.
ISBN: 979-8-218-79581-8

To anyone who thinks life is a struggle.

> "Do not lay up for yourselves treasures on earth, where moth and rust destroy and where thieves break in and steal; but lay up for yourselves treasures in heaven, where neither moth nor rust destroys and where thieves do not break in and steal. For where your treasure is, there your heart will be also."
>
> Matthew 6:19-21[2]

Table of Contents

Preface

1. a Pious Deception	1
Law & a Moral Order	8
the End of Reason	15
2. Jerusalem	25
Heaven & Hell	30
Israel & Zion	31
3. the Messiah	39
4. the Body Politic	45
the People vs. the Crown	55
a Self-Determined Nation	59
5. the Eucharist	63
6. Freedom	69

Table of Contents

7. the Human Struggle   79
    Temptation   82
    Sin   83
    the Marriage Contract   89

8. the Eternal Spirit   97
    Agape   106
    the Human Character   107

9. the Intercession of Mary   119

10. Doubt   129
    God & Mammon   135
    the Eye of the Needle   138
    the Root of Evil   140

11. Alchemy   143
    Magick or Alchemy of the Mind   152

12. the Existential Capitalist   155
    Intellectuals & the Printing Press   160
    the Political Economy   165
    Capital & Capitalism   173
    the Road to Serfdom   177

Table of Contents

―― Monetary History ――

13. the Golden Dream	187
Weights & Measures	190
Timeline of that Other Metal	191
14. China	199
15. Parliament & Democracy	205
Inflating Away the Debt	218
16. 'MMT'	223
the 'Great Society'	245
Conclusion	251
the Future is Artificial	253
Index	
Acknowledgments	
Bibliography	

Preface

People have always sought ways of storing anything of value in a safe place. Whether it was a sentimental item, something salable or currency that could be easily exchanged for goods and services. With money being the most liquid of assets, there has always been a need for banks. As such, economies required an institution that would keep safe the compensation of the persons or businesses which, as the foundation of the economy, create its value.

As I began to research my theory of a Christian monetary system, I came to realize it is extremely rare to say banking is faith based even if we should know it is. It involves promises, trust and honor. What could be more Christian? However, it is never recommended that banking should be treated like a religious institution. Quite the opposite. Since many Christians associate money with materialism, they might prefer not to think of banking as part of a greater spiritual union. However, banks are still considered practical and necessary as a safe store of what we put our faith in even if they are secular and not Christian.

Preface

Despite the fact we take for granted a monetary system, most people with excess income would be reluctant to call banking an industry. Yet, it is. Banks depend on attracting the only source from which it has a purpose: labor and the value produced by labor in an economy. Deposits in accounts represent compensation received for someone's effort to provide for themselves and their families.

Today's reality may not be the same as it once was. I believe when elemental metals were taken away and replaced, man-made currencies obligated banks and ourselves to serve a different master, a questionable monopoly who wants us to believe debt is freedom while promoting faith in greater quantities of credit. They oppose any system that might make it impossible for them to issue more debt and frighten people into thinking we will all be worse off if we don't continue down the same unsustainable path we have been on for way too long. I developed my theory in response to questionable decisions made in the past and why I feel we may want to re-consider their effect on the present and the future.

This book is divided into two sections: the first is religion and spirituality; the second is history. The first section ends with the title of the book. For the sake of brevity, the historical section has been condensed and distilled into four parts. Although I am aware of gold's preferential treatment and status within society and the monetary system, I don't ignore other metals. In order to avoid being labeled a fixated gold-bug, I deliberately prefaced the historical section with a chapter and timeline on the long reign of silver. I then discuss ninth century China during the Yuan dynasty; the British empire and its aristocratic 'Golden Dream', and finally across the Atlantic to the proletarian democracy in the United States. I eventually focus more attention on the United States and its current monetary system since the US has been the de facto leader in the global economy since the end of the Second World War. Its currency is the most common reserve currency and has led the way in creating for the very first time in world history, a global superpower with a 'singular monetary faith' in paper.

While most historians choose political, social or even economic lenses to interpret the past, I have made use of a Christian view. Although I tried to write in depth, a few chapters may deserve a lot more detail, so for the moment, it might be best to consider them merely summaries of potentially future publications.

I should warn readers my view of history is quite revisionist. I am not a historian and although I started writing mostly from memory, I realized I would need research. My research however was lazy in the sense it mostly consisted of internet searches. How accurate the most reliable sources are on the internet is anyone's guess. Even they have their dead links and questionable sources.

Although I started with the thought in mind of not writing anything authoritative, I realized my theory was surprisingly neither rare nor mainstream, it was non-existent! I have since improved a lot of the text and added an index. Because of this, I recommend the index and browsing the same as a cross-reference of themes and ideas between chapters.

The assumption is made that the reader has some previous knowledge of Christianity and/or economics. I won't say secular and non-secular are always in conflict with one another but it's best to point out like oil and water, opposites don't always mix too well without an emulsifier. However, since they are rarely studied together, perhaps an interest in either one will not make a barrier insurmountable without a better understanding of the common ingredient of faith being essential to both within the context of a monetary system.

Finally, being heavily laden with subjective opinion, which chapter might affect common sensibilities is unknown. If anything does, then I have perhaps succeeded in creating the foundation of the discourse I intended. ☺

the Existential Capitalist

❖

a Discourse on Christian Monetary Theory

a Pious Deception

Believe it or not, I find it difficult to define the word religion. Some say it is a philosophy or a code of ethics, morals or an explanation of a greater being's purpose. I have even heard it called politicized spirituality. For the sake of my theory of a better monetary system, I define Christianity as guidance by Christ and faith in the eternal Spirit.

However, while understanding my theory of a Christian monetary system, I believe it is just as important to understand how from a young age I was taught religion.

The religion of the Jews, specifically in the context of Christ's life in Judea was called the Law. A code of instructions as well as guidance for a social order that included histories of creation, human origin, God's benevolence, anger, commandments and, most important of all, judgment. It was also the source of decision making in government. Government was not in a senate, parliament or a congress, but in a place of social congregation usually reserved for pious worship, the Temple in Jerusalem.

The law of the Jews was based almost exclusively on the first five books of the Old Testament called the Torah. Because the Torah is essentially ancient writings collected over centuries, its consistency and accuracy are often called into question. That is to say, how much of it is historical fact and how much of it is literature? Because the influence of the law, and perhaps secular law, is the ability to convince enough of a majority of the validity of an argument that it becomes legislated. And what better way is there to win an argument than using Biblical history? The truth is we have created a false narrative: a fiction. Knowing what in scripture is historical and what is literature is paramount to better governance since humans can be taught, convinced or tricked into believing either fact or fiction is the source of what we might call truth.

How I understand law is that there are three separate categories; there is legislated or Roman law, there is common[1] law and law based on precedent. Different sides (parties) can use one, the other or all of them as they wish in order to gain an advantage with their argument. Legislative law or written law is how a rule has been codified and cannot usually be altered easily or on a whim. Legislative law is perhaps the easiest to defend, but it is the most difficult to oppose. On the other hand, Common law is a bit more flexible in the sense that makes use of a well-structured argument and is often based on personal opinion. Precedent is simply consideration of previous judgments made on a similar case.

---

[1] English family law; an alternate to Roman (legislated) or precedent.

That said, one must also be aware that sometimes parties in opposition can prefer an argument based on one or the other type of law. If one side preferred Mosaic[1] arguments, the other might have countered with the wisdom of Solomon[2].

> 'Then some of the Sadducees, who deny that there is a resurrection, came to Him and asked Him, saying: "Teacher, Moses wrote to us that if a man's brother dies, having a wife, and he dies without children, his brother should take his wife and raise up offspring for his brother. Now there were seven brothers. And the first took a wife, and died without children. And the second took her as wife, and he died childless. Then the third took her, and in like manner the seven also; and they left no children, and died. Last of all the woman died also. Therefore, in the resurrection, whose wife does she become? For all seven had her as wife."
>
> 'Jesus answered and said to them, "The sons of this age marry and are given in marriage. But those who are counted worthy to attain that age, and the resurrection from the dead, neither marry nor are given in marriage; nor can they die anymore, for they are equal to the angels and are sons of God, being sons of the resurrection."'
>
> Luke 20:27-36[2]

The Sadducees were impressed with Christ's answer, more than likely because both sides were brought up with a common sense view of the law. Christ's answer was a form and substance of what Sadducees would like to hear. I believe it might have been an answer to moral issues

---

[1] Moses; leader of the Exodus. [2] Biblical king who built the first Temple in Jerusalem.

affecting law legislation could not resolve. However, the conservatives, if it is fair to call them that, seemed to have hesitated. Perhaps Christ's criticism of other Jews made them question his loyalty to his own heritage. If so, the question they asked became a test of conservative tradition. The only answer Christ could give would be an answer they already had in mind. I am sure they were relieved to hear what he had to say. Does this passage reveal they had a common ground with Christ even if his belief was in the Spirit and theirs was the wisdom of Solomon?

The other party in the Temple, the Pharisees, were a very different group. I believe they were less guided by wisdom, ancient or otherwise. They were Mosaic. And being Mosaic meant they were guided by Moses and so believed in something similar to Roman codified and legislated law similar to the tablets and the commandments. So, answers without respect to what was written in stone by God or God's will, from an apparently supernatural or metaphysical source was going to be treated with suspicion.

How could anyone, if we believe only in our mortal being in this physical world, Christ included, prove the source of their belief? What is faith made of? How much does it weigh? What form does it have? Although Christ knows Jewish tradition well, the Pharisees doubt he respects the Law, perhaps because they are afraid to believe in a Spirit separate and independent of God because it represents judgment on Earth much as their commandments.

> "Then Jesus spoke to the multitudes and to His disciples, saying: "The scribes and the Pharisees sit in Moses' seat. Therefore whatever they tell you to observe, that observe and do, but do not do according to their works; for they say, and do not do. For they bind heavy burdens, hard to bear, and lay them on men's shoulders; but they themselves will not move them with one of their fingers. But all their works they do to be seen by men. They make their phylacteries broad and enlarge the borders of their garments. They love the best places at feasts, the best seats in the synagogues, greetings in the marketplaces, and to be called by men, 'Rabbi, Rabbi.'"
>
> Matthew 23:1-12[2]

Christ does not let up. As if there is no depth to his anger, he lays into them again. In fact seven more times in Matthew 23:13-39. Or, as they are known, the Seven Woes, where Christ gives the reason for his contempt.

As the Greeks would say, Philia or friendship, Christ appears to have none. I believe that only through the Spirit can we relate; the one to the other as individuals.

Should we consider the condemnation of Christ as their act of revenge? If so, revenge for what reason? Does the truth make people angry? Whatever objection someone might have, Christ won't suffer for himself and what he believes, he will eventually suffer because of a lack of faith. And what his punishment will be is the result not of those who opposed him, it will be the people who waited for an answer while groups of individuals fought each other for control of the Temple and of Jerusalem, in a civil war that eventually preceded its destruction by the Romans.

Does this mean Christ was put on trial in order to settle a dispute between Pharisees and Sadducees? Was he a political sacrifice; a victim of the system? No. Through resurrection, he was saved (as was Pilate[1] from his fear of insurrection). I believe the real tragedy in all this was a kingdom centered around Jerusalem. Despite the failure to recognize a better faith as its foundation, the real victims I believe were gentiles who have continued to teach and be taught that law is freedom.

The lesson is that without Christ, and Jerusalem destroyed, generation after generation, in the last two thousand years either *Fascist or Zionist** has permeated human consciousness against Christ's guidance and a future kingdom with all the vanity, conceit, hypocrisy and materialist deception to convince anyone to believe only in human authority.

Anyone who believes anything of what a modern day Pharisee or Sadducee preaches, may be in for a big surprise when the foundations of nations reveal themselves for what they are: faith in law. Even if it is not Biblical law, government takes credit away from faith claiming to create freedom. If that faith is Christian, it is both a sin and a blasphemy because it is a denial of the Spirit. And when the faith of the people that gives them their authority begins to

---

[1] Roman governor of Judea. * Comprehensive entries are in the Index.

weaken, few may know it as a failed monetary system because we were not taught wisdom and precedent; meaning the wisdom of a Christian faith and the disastrous historical precedent of the insidious nature of debt.

≈ LAW & A MORAL ORDER ≈

When discussing the moral aspect of religion, many discussions do not treat Christianity as it were a separate religion, they make it a philosophical moral addendum to the Jewish religion. This might have led to the idea that separate authority cannot exist, since human nature is impossible to legislate.

Then what is religion's purpose? Can faith in the Spirit benefit both Church and government?

From the perspective of Richard Whately's book *Introductory Lessons on Morals*, the English writer William Paley's philosophy appears to form the basis of Victorian morality. While researching my theory, I kept in mind the idea that attempts to legislate moral behavior have been either productive and conducive to prosperity or repressive of human nature when considering Christianity in relation to the monetary system.

If Whately's commentary of Paley's theory didn't replace Paley's philosophy with something more Christian, did it offer a better view for Jew and Christian? What conclusion did fellow Anglican Thomas Malthus have for stock-broker and good friend, David Ricardo?

> "The advocate for the perfectibility of man, and of society, retorts on the defender of establishments a more than equal contempt. He brands him as the slave of the most miserable and narrow prejudices; or as the defender of the abuses of civil society only because he profits by them."

Someone might call it objective. I call it cynical. Success in those days must have meant preaching the weaknesses of an institution rather than its strengths. Or were they referring to another denomination rather than their own? Even today, any advice from a member of a Church is treated like the start of a clerical conspiracy. However, the worst advice from a politician is always excused by their selfless concern for the well-being of others.

Paley's Watchmaker theory of the universe proves divine creation when we consider the movement of planets is like the movements in a watch. However Paley believes the source of sin is our physical being. Whately narrows the vague anatomical approach to something more focused on physically intimate or as he references Paul in scripture and 1 Corinthians 3:3[1]:

> "For ye are yet carnal: for whereas there is among you envying, and strife, and divisions, are ye not carnal, and walk as men?"

Rather than state explicitly that sex is sin, Whately, like Paley seems to imply that without Christ, we are not upright civilized humans, we are beasts. Instead of offending Victorian moral sensibilities, he offers reconciliation in lessons of virtue and obligation. If Whately had been so exact about the source of sin, what effect would such a precise definition have had? Would the more progressive 19th century proletarian[1] have been offended at such a broad condemnation of human desire? Did such a revisionist view of scripture provoke a reactionary rejection of religious authority and a preference for secular guidance instead?

[1] Secular working-class labor.

Whately mentions Aristotle and makes frequent use of the word duty in his book *Introductory Lessons on Morals*. He mentions Aristotle's *Ethics* but not in the context of Aristotle's belief that the individual is subordinate to the state. Because the Church is founded on voluntary service and association, pleasure and pain theories of human motive clash with Whately's idea of obligation and duty that cannot be from any source other than the Old Testament.

If Whately is expounding a virtuous and just government then he does so without anything I would call spiritual. Government is a necessity for social order. Even the most anti-establishment anarchist would find a nation without order to be impossible to manage or exist for very long. So that leaves me wondering what is an Archbishop in the Church of England's best course away from sin if not the law and the manipulation of opinion with a system of reward, punishment, threats and promises?

> "For Man's moral faculty is (as was observed at the beginning) capable, like our other faculties, cultivation and improvement and liable also to be depraved and perverted in various ways. And a moral instructor is one who undertakes not indeed to create a moral faculty in a Being quite destitute of it (any more than an oculist undertakes to create eyes), but to cultivate and improve the moral faculty and remove its imperfections, and preserve it from corruption; even as an oculist seeks to preserve the eyes and to cure the diseases of them."

Whately does give some good advice. God is our source of morality and is obedience to Divine Will. With better judgment, humans have conscience and motives. The New

Testament does not, unlike the Old Testament provide rules. Better judgment is not human, it is an attribute of God. I would only add that better judgment is why a crown is on the head of a monarch – it is a symbol of faith in Christ.

> *"One may illustrate the distinct uses of Scripture in all that relates to morals and of natural Conscience, by the comparison of a sun dial and a clock. The clock has the advantage of being always at hand, to be consulted at any hour of the day or night; while the dial is of use only when the sun shines on it But then the clock is liable to go wrong, and vary from the true time; and it has no power in itself of correcting its own errors; so that these may go on increasing, to any extent unless it be from time to time regulated by the dial, which is alone the unerring guide."*

This is an excellent metaphor and a play on the use of the word sun (Son) being a better guide than any human invention of any kind, even if it is also practical and useful. This is particularly the case in point with Paley and his idea of the 'cosmic chronograph' model of the universe.

However, did Whately misinterpret Matthew 10:5-7[1]?

> *These twelve Jesus sent forth, and commanded them, saying, "Go not into the way of the Gentiles, and into any city of the Samaritans enter ye not: But go rather to the lost sheep of the house of Israel. And as ye go, preach, saying, 'The kingdom of heaven is at hand.'"*

If we are brought together by law, Jew or gentile, how does Christianity bring together both anyone without faith? If the difference is between consensus and the individual, it is impossible to offer the law as an answer to both; unless of course the difference is a solution to the Struggle. Unfortunately, Christianity appears to only offering judgment for our sins. This leads to the conclusion that someone must abandon their belief in any single authority solution and accept any number of denominations.

Whately tries to clear up the confusion with the idea that Jewish scripture is something left over from the infancy of religion and Christianity is its moral superior.

> "Hence, the gospel, which was designed for men in a more advanced state than that of the ancient Israelites, gives much less of precise directions than the Mosaic law. It is not that a less degree of moral excellence is required of the Christian, but that the gospel lays down pure and elevated moral principles, rather than exact rules; and requires men to conform their lives to those principles."

However, we should be more wary of false prophets in the Christian religion than anywhere else.

> "But what helps to mislead people as to this point is, that we may often see what appear to be virtuous habits quite unconnected with each other. For instance, a man who is sober, from being convinced that intemperance would bring sickness, and perhaps poverty, may appear to be practicing the virtue of temperance; and yet he may be a cheat, and a liar, etc."

This statement is true. As relates to government and religion, it should be acknowledged that a man may be a thoroughly morally upstanding being who is judged to be free of every sin but knowingly, under threat of punishment, is in contempt and disregard of every law and legal judgment. I don't mean to condone any illegal acts or suggest Christianity does the same. In order to make my example objective I must include the exact opposite as well. A man might never have broken a single law and yet be the most immoral person on the planet. I believe what is moral and what is lawful rarely overlap, how we define them does.

Unfortunately, Whately does not confer on the Church any greater practical authority than the government has with the law. He believes the Church, like government, is apt to faults caused by human frailty. If we accept human nature is by definition sinful then I assume this is why preference was given to non-Christians to make decisions about faith as it relates to banking and the monetary system. This left the population free to live without an oppressive burden imposed on them while the dirty business of government was taken care of by a marginalized minority. Thus suffered the Jews our sense of guilt and shame while we were made happy Christians knowing Christ died for us and our sins!

Whately's saving grace has to be his comment on the proverbial golden rule in Matthew 7:12, commonly translated as *'Do unto others as you would have them do unto you.'*

If we choose to accept we are burdened by judgment and judgment is faith in an eternal substance which men or mankind cannot create, we accept guidance by that which is eternal. If however, we refuse eternal in favor of that which is created by men or mankind, then we must be blind to the detrimental effect it has on the economy. There is only one way to describe this: democracy is the lowest common denominator in consensus. The greater the majority, the more opposition is made humble and the more consensus flatters what is human. Unfortunately, a majority conspiring to commit an infraction, moral or otherwise, does not make it right. This is just as true in law as in faith.

❧ THE END OF REASON ❧

"If a man receives circumcision on the Sabbath, so that the law of Moses should not be broken, are you angry with Me because I made a man completely well on the Sabbath?"

John 7:23[2]

The reader will probably be wondering how I made circumcision a part of monetary theory. When discussing Christ in Judea, it is impossible. Although conspiracy theorists on the internet might disagree, I believe Zionists, not Jews took control of banking in the 19th century. In doing so, they sought to fulfill a purpose of removing the idea of eternal judgment from supposedly Christian nations and instead imposing a rule of secular law. Circumcision was simply a part of accepting the conversion.

Making banking public rather than private is because generations had been instructed that money was not just the root of evil, it was a source of guilt and shame. To make matters worse, it was materialistic and anyone who believed otherwise was not worthy of a greater moral purpose. If we examine the portrayal of Jews prior to the 20th century, the stereotypes were less than flattering. Any non-Christian could get the blame if a failure in the faith based monetary system meant judgment. However, what if pious members of institutional religion, thinking themselves more understanding of faith resisted and in doing so they became anti-Christian?

Shakespeare's 16th century portrayal of Shylock in *The Merchant of Venice* was a surprising commentary on the fact that so many Italian families during the Middle Ages were involved in finance and yet after 1500, were gradually being replaced by Northern Europeans, many of whom were Jewish. I believe uncertainty about a Christian purpose developed from the fact becoming clear of who for what purpose controlled wealth and capital. Did Shylock care if he lost some of his money, with his demand for a "pound of flesh"? How successful would Antonio have been to woo Portia if he lost his case and the ability to consummate an intimate relationship? Was a Jew threatening Antonio with a figurative loss of manhood that he himself had already suffered? Shakespeare's play certainly has some interesting subtext if we choose to consider it a commentary on financial castration.

It seems obvious that Zionists should manage human nature and the source of sin. Letting what I refer to as 'gentile Jews' or 'Old Testament Christians' be responsible for a system of materialism and greed was a sort of reactionary racism; a conflict of breeding; acceptable to anyone who believed religion made them morally superior, yet were fair enough to apply laws establishing equanimity among their communities.

We should refrain from contempt of institutional religion and accept, as we should, that there has been an attempt in the last few centuries to create Universal Government, more so by gentiles than anyone else. That is because of the confusion that Zionist means Jew. That couldn't be further from the truth. Israel exists today because of the participation of many more gentiles.

So while the Mark of the Beast generally refers to a number from Revelation 13:8, I propose considering the somewhat recent promotion of circumcision. Circumcision is the rite of passage for a young male infant to be a Jew. It is both a requirement and a permanent sign of membership in a nation. Although gentiles have made female circumcision illegal by labeling it genital mutilation, male circumcision since the Second World War has been allowed to continue with the consent of the medical establishment as a perceived health benefit.

However, whether we agree or not to any particular race or religion to be tasked with a particular purpose in any nation or any part of the world, I believe circumcision has a deep and lasting effect on the psyche of the male gender. Psychologists have determined that the pain felt by an infant is remembered the rest of their life as a sort of primal pain. A pain that in turn might affect gender identity and mature intimate relationships.

Because of the dominant role of the mother in childhood development, equally important to both male and female, the male child who is circumcised may direct blame toward the maternal rather than the paternal. Because circumcision occurs in less than a week after birth, it is not a conscious memory. The child may grow into an adult with feelings of inadequacy and an anger left unresolved. In more serious cases, it may result in a resentment of the female gender and a type of castration anxiety.

This is particularly tragic among Jews since their society is matrilineal. After circumcision, a child and then the adult may develop passive-aggressive tendencies and an incomplete or poor understanding of their own character. I believe Gentiles who suffer this treatment may also fail in gender development so that they develop a less than ideal concept of spirituality within the framework of a Christian education.

While I believe civilized society should prevent genital mutilation in all infants, it is often allowed for medical reasons that can rarely if ever be proved. Likewise, justifying it because it is the answer to immoral behavior is in itself immoral. Believing it appropriate because Christ was circumcised is a defeatist approach and we should be relieved if we are not. So that we have a better understanding of Christian guidance and the Spirit, it should not be allowed.

However, if it is not tolerated, then we would have to consider which is worse: denying a nation the ritual of removing from an infant a piece of flesh fused to their genitals; not being loose as it is after adolescence; peeled off, much like a nail might be removed from a finger. If they refuse, would we have to limit their residence in a Christian land? Probably not.

History shows, if anyone truly believes in their people and their beliefs, they would willingly choose to go somewhere else rather accept an intolerance of their most sacred customs and traditions. Migration is what tribes have been doing since the dawn of man. The best example of this truth was the show-down between religion and government and the refusal of Lionel de Rothschild in 1850 to make a vow including Christ on the New Testament before taking his place as a democratically elected member of Parliament. Although he was asked to leave when he did not agree to the wording in the vow, Parliament eventually passed the Jewish Relief Act in 1858 which removed the barrier to his faith. Any embarrassment or humiliation felt by anyone involved may have been alleviated by a title and a place in the House of Lords in 1885.

What a quiet revolution the Conversion of 1858 was. If a republic was what Britain wanted then it would not be inhibited by a disinterested monarch. Why would a queen intervene on a matter of faith when she would be defending scripture written by men, mostly about men and intended for men? After all, when her husband passed, Victoria left most decisions in Parliament to her prime ministers.

Rothschild's steadfast refusal was a test of our own faith. His was a noble act that should have been admired and respected. It is true a human may swear to something and not know what it means; going through the motions in order to achieve some perceived ambition. How many thoughts in our mind only exist so that we find a common ground with each other even if we question the validity of what we repeat to ourselves and each other over and over?

However, allowing a non-Christian into government was to admit that Anglican understanding of Christianity was superficial and vain and we are hollow men. I ask myself if a man is wealthier and therefore must be wiser, then what could a gentile fear if someone eventually put Christianity and the monetary system together? There should have a refusal on principle even if all we remember is that Christ was an answer to morality. Legal consensus and committee will never be an answer to sin unless we agree to defend the eternal Spirit and continue to believe Christ guides our mortal salvation.

We should not forget the root cause of anti-Semitic friction and the Crucifixion. Even if we believe the Resurrection proved eternal life, many of the devout still feel a bitterness toward the people of Jerusalem for a decision made by the Sanhedrin. If the Anglican religion was a reformed Catholicism then perhaps it was time to compromise and find unity in purpose. Or was it?

If we understand the expulsion of the Jews from England in 1290, and not being allowed to return until 1656, was primarily an act of monetary economics then historical fact makes more sense. Christians could never be made slaves for too much debt and a government could never fail their people with a bad faith. If governments divide individuals from guidance by the Spirit and offer the law as a poor substitute, nations are united by a common enemy even if the enemy is our sin. Christianity and sin cannot be made to work together.

Today, however, I believe we are united with the sin of denial. It would be almost impossible to create legislation opposed to circumcision without some sort of exception on religious grounds. Since Victorian times, as many gentiles as Jews have adopted this practice as their own so much so that more gentiles in their numbers in the US and Europe are circumcised. It would be a tragic historical fact if appearing to be ending discrimination, Britain instead created a bias against Christ, putting an end to the idea of Christian authority in the future.

Despite political correctness in the world today, will history make this world any better? Rather than seeming to punish ourselves for believing we could be united without Christian faith is to know a gate has been opened.

It may be worth mentioning Whately had this to say in 1857 in his *Lessons on Morals*:

> "It is a proverbial remark, and a just one, that 'a liar will sometimes repeat the same falsehood so often, that at last he will come to believe it himself.' He did not originally say it because he believed it; but, by saying it, has brought himself to believe it."
>
> "For when any country (according to the illustration above given) has long permitted rebellious subjects to disobey the legitimate governors, and transgress the laws, it is likely that

in time those rebels will themselves become the real governors, and will make such laws as they please."

If dragons exist and have been let loose and they continue to plague us all, how much more difficult will it be to contain them if we don't understand why they were set free in the first place?

While discussing faith in government, it is worth mentioning something not available in the 1850s – the establishment of a psychoanalytic school of thought. I refer to the most well-known theorist Sigmund Freud[1] and his theory of human development; in particularly the oral, anal and genital stages. Freud said that from birth to adolescence, humans progress through various stages of development. Something I have noticed as an armchair psychologist is a direct correlation between an incomplete understanding of one's gender identity and a fixation. If one stage of development is not completed successfully, a child becoming an adult may not have a complete understanding of their character.

If a symptom of obesity is overeating, a child did not complete the oral stage. Ending breast feeding too early and a human, even when they are older, may continually seek a mother substitute. If the anal stage fails, then someone might have an obsessive compulsive need for cleanliness and hand washing. When the genital stage doesn't complete, someone might develop a fixation from an earlier stage. Too much coddling or even disapproval during any stage may mean issues of self-worth and acceptance.

[1] Austrian psychoanalyst who believed human character was formed from the libido.

There may be hundreds of examples. What my theory suggests is that if anyone suffers a trauma that affects their gender identity, they may in fact develop similar symptoms and become fixated in a previous stage. If so, then the Spirit is not well served. This is because those stages of human development occur within what are known as erogenous zones. I believe they are in a Christian sense not only a part of human development, they can also be a primary source of guilt and shame. Even though they might ostensibly represent reproduction, they can also represent gratification, indulgence and sin.

So, a badly formed character may inhibit a better understanding of what is spiritual and instead only become fixated on what is mortal, material or human. This is why I believe when we needed a better understanding of faith, Zionists were given preference with paper rather than metal. I believe we felt less of a threat thinking of a substance as a fixation rather than anything being an immortal presence. Unfortunately for all of us, there exists a cloud in the silver lining of any nation choosing a Christian faith. It is the conflict within every individual of both fear and desire contained within judgment.

I conclude from what Christ says in John 7:23, we can never heal from circumcision that is imposed on us. However, in 7:24[2] Christ reminds us: *"Do not judge according to appearance, but judge with righteous judgment."*

Jerusalem

The region of Judea before the birth of Christ was a kingdom of a people waiting for an answer. Anyone before the birth of Christ, who believed in an answer to the Struggle, did not know one. They did not have the future Messiah promised in scripture.

However, instead of affirming or refuting the Law of the Old Testament, Christ brought an answer to individual life, its meaning and knowing the difference between right and wrong; a moral order so vital to a people who attempted consensus with what they had already been given by God. If we believe scripture thus far did not provide an answer to everything, we should accept Christ brought an additional faith. However, the faith of the people before Christ was in what was called the Old Covenant, a belief that the Law was given exclusively to the Jews. Although Christ's birth was the beginning of a New Covenant, Christ would have to defend himself against accusations of trying to replace the Covenant. And he occasionally appeared to express his frustration at the slightest suggestion.

Jerusalem

> *"O Jerusalem, Jerusalem, the one who kills the prophets and stones those who are sent to her! How often I wanted to gather your children together, as a hen gathers her chicks under her wings, but you were not willing!"*
>
> Matthew 23:37[2]

Christ could either be lamenting the loss of the physical city or Jerusalem's unwillingness to convert. He could also have been saddened over his own lack of success in being able to convert its people.

> *"Then Jesus went out and departed from the temple, and His disciples came up to show Him the buildings of the temple. And Jesus said to them, 'Do you not see all these things? Assuredly, I say to you, not one stone shall be left here upon another, that shall not be thrown down.'"*
>
> Matthew 24:1-2[2]

However Christ feels about the capitol of Judea – Jerusalem, he seems relatively unconcerned about the loss of the center of its social organization – the Temple. It is even possible to sense his anger as he appears to so accurately predict its destruction.

Jerusalem was a divided city before Christ as people sought to validate authority given to them by God in ancient scripture. However, even though they were on the same page, figuratively speaking, human nature being what it is, consensus could be extremely difficult when it came to decision making.

> "Now as He drew near, He saw the city and wept over it, saying, 'If you had known, even you, especially in this your day, the things that make for your peace! But now they are hidden from your eyes. For days will come upon you when your enemies will build an embankment around you, surround you and close you in on every side, and level you, and your children within you, to the ground; and they will not leave in you one stone upon another, because you did not know the time of your visitation.'"
>
> Luke 19:41-44[2]

I believe tears can reveal truth or lies. The truth was the loss. The lie is that the world has learned its lesson. It should be noted, Christ is not condemning Jerusalem, he is cursing its fate. Christ is angry while trying to save a government, business and social center. However he might appear, either a sad depressed human or a savior frustrated by resistance, we must come to our own conclusions. What we do know is Christ predicted Jerusalem's fate in 70 AD. And that was tragic, because I believe its destruction represented the end rather than the beginning of better spiritual guidance and unity in faith. This event was made even more tragic by the fact that a heritage disappeared. The fate of Jerusalem was the end of a lineage that predates records. Whether Pharisee or Sadducee, the residents of the 'City of God' may in fact have been the only people in history with a continuous bloodline back to the First Temple.

So, to whom do we apportion blame?

Jerusalem's fate might have been set in stone if intervention was the only option for the Roman Forum against a perceived threat when the people of Judea could not resolve their internal conflict.

According to first century historian Josephus, Jerusalem was already in violent upheaval before the arrival of Titus[1]. Is it possible Rome's intervention was an attempt to save a divided city from itself or could conflict have been the result of a failure to understand Christ's message of eternal life?

Consider the multiple possible interpretations of Matthew 27:25[1]. Who in that verse and chapter might have been afraid of eternal judgment and felt condemned by someone other than human authority when they raised their voices to Pilate, the Roman governor?

> 'All the people answered "May his blood be on us and on our children!"'

Of the political parties in Jerusalem that we know of from scripture, did they all disappear after Jerusalem's destruction? Although no one calls themselves a Herodian, Pharisee, or Sadducee, they have parallels in current political organizations. If you are under government contract, you live off the tax payer, therefore a Herodian. A

[1] Roman military leader and later Caesar.

Republican could be labeled a worshiper of money, a modern-day Pharisee. What about governance and law? Are Democrats Sadducees?

With their ideological anti-elitist focus on a strong middle class, is either party any different? A democratic decision was made when Pilate 'washed his hands' and let the people decide. It could be said the crucifixion was the result of a popular referendum even if I believe it was a kangaroo court of hearsay and scant evidence. The accused was not well represented. And the jury of his peers, if there was one, was a hysterical mob.

Despite the Biblical lesson on how to improve sovereign guidance, I believe Christ was gambling on his wisdom making a better world when, given enough time, European nations chose a political solution to the risk of unmanageable levels of debt.

❧ HEAVEN & HELL ☙

  The reason the crucifixion should be discussed in detail is because I believe a punishment should fit a crime. Christ was given a place reserved for a common thief for what occurred in Gethsemane[1]. He took the place of a thief yet was condemned next to others who were not like him, resurrected. I think we should consider the literal position of the crucifixion, the place where Christ was put to death.

Jerusalem, often referred to as the City of God would have been entirely inappropriate for such an event. Why was Golgotha more appropriate? Because I believe it was the middle ground between good and evil. If the City of God was heaven, then where was the dark side of human nature; a place where society's secrets were sent; a place of despair and judgment; a place where desperate souls erased unpalatable memories? Not to be confused with what the Greeks called Hades. Definitely not a place ruled over by an Olympian God. This was Gehenna[2].

I believe from my research Gehenna was quite simply a rubbish dump that burned day and night outside the walls. I imagine if the wind was in the right direction on a clear day, clouds of dark sooty smoke passing over Jerusalem; on a bad day, the acrid stench being almost too much to bear. The proverbial lake of fire where disease was cured, crimes resolved and sins forgotten. Was it an answer to social order and a moral cleansing or was it a place where there will be no re-birth and no resurrection and therefore no favorable judgment and no eternal life?

[1] Matthew 26:36-46. [2] Gehenna or Gehennom translate as Hell or Hell-like.

❧ ISRAEL & ZION ☙

It is impossible to mention Israel today without discussing Biblical history and the Zionist[1] movement of the 19th century.

I was brought up with the impression Biblical Israel was a kingdom, yet in scripture Moses does not appear to be a monarchist. He is a class-based hero. If I believe faith guides a kingdom, then why become Zion? Israel became a democratic state in 1948 because of race and religion, not despite race and religion. Now we find ourselves in a awkward situation where anyone who dares to challenge a false historical narrative with what is in scripture is accused of reviving centuries old anti-semitism by none other than a united front of both Fascists and Zionists who not so long ago appeared to be sworn enemies!

Zionism started in Europe among people afraid of losing their ethnic heritage and cultural identity. They wanted to re-establish their lineage back to either the Biblical First or historical Second Temple. Despite the nomadic Sephardic Jews of North Africa, the eastern Mizrahi or the more narrow regional Yemenite Jews; those whose proximity to Judea might have made them more likely descended from the time after Jerusalem's destruction, that presented a problem for the intended goal in mind of European Zionists.

Let's not forget that the 'Gathering' in Deuteronomy 30:1-5 should have been the restoration of a kingdom some believe

---

[1] Jewish repatriation in the Holy Lands.

would have only occurred after the arrival of a Messiah who a great number of people believe was Christ in the New Testament. We should also not forget that the Gathering refers to the Babylonian captivity and not the Diaspora[1] which occurred much later after Christ. What the Zionists were attempting in the 19th century was the restoration of a monarchy which had already occurred in Judea under the Romans and had no justifiable reason for another attempt.

However, I believe if the Resurrection has any meaning then we should make use of what we can from scripture pending another crisis affecting the monetary system re-affirming our conviction a better world is possible with faith in our mortal being and another cult of personality.

> "Let the sovereignty be granted us over a portion of the globe large enough to satisfy the reasonable requirements of a nation; the rest we shall manage for ourselves."
>
> Theodor Herzl
> *A Jewish State* (1896)

The truth was Zionists in the 19th century might have been divided over the issue, yet still found favor with many high-level individuals among Anglo-Israel societies.[2] Even with one-hundred percent support, Zionist Israel would have been so fragmented in trying to find a peaceful solution to opposition from much larger Muslim and Arabic nations. Gentile support became an absolutely necessity.

---

[1] The global dispersion of Jews after Jerusalem's destruction.
[2] A discussion of Israelism is beyond the scope of this book.

Zionists could argue with all they had intellectually. Unfortunately, political compromise can only go so far. The pen may be mightier than the sword, until you need a sword. So, Zionists had to recruit gentiles to fight for them, which they did; middle-class converts from bourgeois liberalism joining with their national-socialist working class brethren. When led with the deluded idea that the law of any nation, not just Israel, could secure or even unite a global empire, a recipe for mass hysteria was complete.

Were either of these men Zionist?

Theodor Herzl, the de facto leader of the 19th century Zionist movement, took it on himself to follow German Kaiser Wilhelm II (*left image*) on a state visit to Jerusalem in 1898 and supposedly asked him to request concessions from Turkish Sultan Abdul Hamid II (*right image*) related to settlement in Palestine. I don't believe that it would have been politically expedient for the Kaiser to honor such a request, especially considering the Sultan's objection to foreign immigration was a well known historical fact. Added to the fact was the Austro-German Alliance of 1879, whether ostensibly to protect against Russia, placed Austria on a precarious 'front line' with the Ottoman empire.

Despite an incredible level of naïveté, Herzl clearly states who he believes will answer their call:

> "England, mighty England, free England, with its world-embracing outlook, will understand us and our aspirations. With England as a starting point we may be sure that the Zionist idea will soar further and higher than ever before."

Fourth Congress Address, 1900

Even with the support of the world's biggest empire, there were still doubts in his mind.

> "You know that many have tried their hand at this task which confronts us, animated by good intentions and moreover with great material means at their disposal. But you also know that these attempts came to nothing. Why? Because they all set out from a false premise. They said: 'In the beginning is money.' No! In the beginning is the idea! Money will secure hirelings, but it will not arouse a people. Only an idea will bring this to pass. And it has brought it to pass."

Fifth Congress Address, 1901

Without the generous support of large donations, millions would not equal success. Apparently, a well-ordered migration to Palestine was going to prove difficult.

Jerusalem

> *"The means which are to be devoted to our national aim cannot be utilized for other purposes through the caprice or mistakes of individuals. This financial institution must be directed according to the rules laid down by the Congress and with the care of a good, scrupulous pater familias. And now that it is in existence we can proceed to the execution of the plan which our late friend, Professor Schapira, of the University of Heidelberg, presented to the First Congress: the creation of a National Fund. The money will be deposited in the Jewish Colonial Trust in London."*

Fifth Congress Address, 1901

The truth is the Trust was actually a lending bank making loans for purchases of land in Palestine. Unfortunately, no purchases could be made if no one was willing to sell. Even Baron de Hirsch[1] refused to use any of his phenomenal wealth on Herzl's fanciful idea. So how did Zionism eventually succeed?

Should we consider perhaps a seed was planted and the roots of conflict took hold in faith while we look for a reason to finance a war after we were told it had to have been the assassination of the next in line to the throne of the Austro-Hungarian empire?

What about a war to remove a ruling class, and another deliberately stoked with anti-Semitism that would create a secular proletarian establishment only if gentiles could be convinced they should lead the way?

---

[1] Philanthropist who often supported Jewish causes.

> "It would be an excellent idea to call in respectable, accredited anti-Semites as liquidators of property. To the people they would vouch for the fact that we do not wish to bring about the impoverishment of the countries that we leave. At first they must not be given large fees for this; otherwise we shall spoil our instruments and make them despicable as 'stooges of the Jews.' Later their fees will increase, and in the end we shall have only Gentile officials in the countries from which we have emigrated. The anti-Semites will become our most dependable friends, the anti-Semitic countries our allies."

The Complete Diaries of ..., Vol. 1

After Hamid was deposed in 1908 by liberal intellectuals in his own government, they don't appear to have been any more amenable to the idea of foreign occupation of Palestine. On the other hand, defending Europe from any Turkish expansion might have meant German annexation of a considerable amount of Habsburg[1] territory. I believe the British may have been somewhat concerned a Catholic front line with Islam would hold. Even though the last of the Crusades was in the 13th century, we shouldn't ignore the influence of historical precedent in national unity, hence England's declaration of war against Germany in 1914 after the death of Archduke Ferdinand.

Germany would attempt to regain some dignity in the 1930s by militarizing their economy and mobilizing in an effort to annex Poland much to the chagrin of Britain yet again, who summarily declared another war.

---

[1] Last of the major European Catholic monarchies.

Jerusalem

While Hitler* attempted an alliance with the British Empire in a concerted effort against the Soviet Union, faith in banking and finance had been making a barely perceptible move across the Atlantic to the United States. After a second war, proletarians assumed control of that faith with the most powerful weapons ever invented. With coffers emptied and nations weak from more than a century of almost continuous conflict, there was an agreement to consensus and Israel was born.

In summary, Israel today is a European political construct meant to serve a universal government. It was the end of monarchies and empires; the beginning of a new monetary standard; a proletarian uprising and a combination of national pride only made possible with gentile effort and sacrifice.

* See Index.

the Messiah

I was brought up with the idea that the Bible was a book that all the other books contained within were a timeline of a historical record written with divine inspiration and some said perfect word of God. I was taught a bias that although Christ was Jewish, the Jews would never understand the New Testament and that only a gentile could make use of what Jews chose not to believe. Even if that was offensive.

Why would making Christ the Messiah be offensive?

The question of whether Jesus of Nazareth – known as Christ – fulfills the role of a Messiah promised in Hebrew Scriptures is one of the most enduring debates in religious history. This chapter will explore both sides of the argument: the Christian claim that Jesus is the Messiah and the Jewish argument that he is not, drawing on historical sources, scriptural analysis, and the dual nature of Biblical texts as both history and literature.

What is the doctrinal Christian argument?

the Messiah

Christianity centers on the belief that Jesus was the Messiah ('anointed one'), foretold by the prophets in the Old Testament. Christians argue that Jesus fulfills specific messianic prophecies, including:

- **His birth in Bethlehem**: Micah 5:2 is interpreted as predicting the Messiah's birth in Bethlehem, fulfilled in Matthew 2:1.

- **He belonged to the lineage of David**: Jeremiah 23:5 foresaw a Messiah from David's line, referenced in Matthew 1:1 and Luke 3:23-38 for both Mary and Joseph.

- **He was a suffering servant**: Zechariah 12:10 & Isaiah 53:5 describes one who is "*pierced for our transgressions*", which Christians believe refers to Jesus' crucifixion (John 19:37).

- **Eternal life**: Psalm 16:10 is interpreted as a prophecy of Christ's resurrection, referenced in Acts 2:31.

Additionally, Jesus' miracles, teachings, and his acceptance of the title 'Messiah' (Matthew 16:16, John 4:26) are seen as evidence of a messianic role.

However, individuals or institutions may be accused of heresy if they reject Jesus as the Messiah.

So, why was Jesus not the Messiah?

the Messiah

When speaking of Christ as the 'anointed one', Christians are referring to the meaning of the word 'Messiah' (Hebrew: מָשִׁיחַ, Mashiach) and its Greek translation 'Christos' (Χριστός). Christ was baptized with water but not strictly speaking 'anointed'. You may be asking yourself what is the meaning of 'anointed one', and the practice of anointing in the Ancient World?

Anointing was the ritual act of pouring oil on someone's head, signifying that the person has been chosen, set apart, or empowered for a special role by God. In ancient Israel, kings, priests, and sometimes prophets were anointed as a sign of divine selection and authority (see, for example, the anointing of King David in 1 Samuel 16:13).

- **Conception theory**: If Christ was conceived in heaven and given a virgin[1] birth, he was not descended from David through a patrilineal lineage with Mary (a female) or Joseph (his legal guardian).

- **Messianic prophecies**: Key prophecies including universal peace (Isaiah 2:4), rebuilding the First Temple (Ezekiel 37:26-28), and worldwide recognition of a monotheistic God (Zechariah 14:9) are still unfulfilled.

- **The nature of the Messiah**: The Jewish Messiah is expected to be a human leader, not divine, who will create a role in Jerusalem of political sovereignty over all nations.

---

[1] This book defines virgin as unmarried; adultery is extra or pre-marital relations; chastity is faith within marriage and celibacy is abstinence.

- **Interpretation of prophecies**: Many learned individuals argue that Christian interpretations of texts like Isaiah 53 refer collectively to Israel, not a single individual.

- **Resurrection and divinity**: Jewish tradition does not include as messianic criteria that which is essential to Christian belief – resurrection or divinity. The Messiah is mortal and not expected to die and rise, nor to be worshipped as God.

If Scripture can be either history or literature, how do we separate fact from fiction?

Modern scholarship often approaches the Bible as both a historical document and a work of literature. This dual perspective raises questions about the factual accuracy and interpretive layers of scripture:

- **A historical record**: Archaeology and historical research confirm some Biblical events, but others are disputed or unverified.

- **A literary construct**: Biblical texts use metaphor, narrative, and theological interpretation, blending history with spiritual meaning.

- **Messianic expectations**: Jewish messianic beliefs evolved over time and were often shaped by adverse historical circumstances, such as exile and oppression.

While Christians offer compelling theological and literary arguments for Jesus as the Messiah, a historical and textual analysis rooted in Jewish tradition finds that he does not fulfill essential criteria. The resurrection and the claim to divine nature, rather than confirming messianic status, place Jesus outside the bounds of traditional Jewish expectations. The Messiah, as envisioned in the Hebrew Scriptures and Jewish thought, was to be a human leader who brings earthly peace and redemption, not a God-like figure whose mission centers on eternal life and salvation.

Therefore, based on historical context, scriptural analysis, and a fact-versus-fiction theory, the Christian concept of the Messiah represents a significant re-interpretation, merging history with theology and literature, but ultimately diverges from the original prophetic vision.

the Body Politic

Although it may appear simple enough, the question I ask myself is: *"What is a church?"* Is it merely a building; a place of congregation, worship, sermons and reverence? I don't think so. I believe a church is an intellectual construct and one exists wherever there is a Christian. If an individual is Christian, then there must exist a church. Therefore, it stands to reason, if there are no Christians, then no church. Because a church is not a building built by humans of any material, it is at its foundation, an understanding of Christ and Christian wisdom. Within a single mind can be built a church, the philosophical association, the metaphor of a building. Even if someone standing on a desolate plot of land in the middle of nowhere is Christian, then there is a church. However, construct a building on that same land, and call it a church, without a single Christian, I believe it cannot be, not in a spiritual sense.

Being Christian means understanding the wisdom of the Christian Way. Because the answer is not Christ or Christ the man Jesus, it is the Spirit and eternal life through the Resurrection.

During his lifetime, members of the first Church were people lucky enough to be taught by Christ himself. They were called disciples, or students. Later, some of them became apostles or teachers themselves. And buildings were constructed and established in his honor. Then knowledgeable individuals held a special position in the Church as bishops and their office was administered from a physical building, a cathedral. However, as much as this seems to have been a natural evolution of a spiritual movement, this Church with human bishops and a cathedral became a political institution. I believe that common thought at the time was that scripture would make better civic service.

So, Christendom, as it was called, was established. It became the Orthodox church during the reign of the emperor Constantine (306-337) in Byzantium, replacing the name with Constantinople. Although the citizens of Byzantium still referred to themselves as Roman, they adopted the Greek language and culture even if today, in order to avoid confusion, it is known as the Byzantine empire. So the Eastern Orthodox Church after the First Council of Nicaea in 325 was the beginning of a unified political Church creating a fragmented and uncertain heritage. Despite disagreement among the early churches, arguments appeared to be somewhat settled with a Biblical canon of scripture itself. Even though the 27 books of the New Testament had been complete since the early second century, the Council of Rome (382) is credited with being first to canonize scripture. The Orthodox church made them part of their canon in the Second Council of Trullan (692). Despite the Gelasian Decree in the sixth century attempting a unilateral authority over the other churches, it should be noted that these 'churches' had not previously 'officially' included the Christian New Testament in their doctrine, only the Old Testament.

Now this is where history and personal opinion diverge. How Christian Constantine was is debatable. Yet, how tolerant he was to any religion after Christianity was made legal with the Edict of Milan in 313 is not at all debatable. I consider this Church as it was established with its five pillars: Alexandria, Antioch, Constantinople, Jerusalem and Rome, a political union.

However, we should not forget that early synagogues allowed Christian congregations. So if the Universal Church is Christian, why does it appear to be very similar to those places of Jewish worship? I think there must be a conspiracy if I believe the purpose of Christianity couldn't be further from the ambition to be a part of any government, Jewish or not. The Christian faith should not condemn nor justify law. If a Christian should participate in politics then let them expose its influence in a domain where it should not exist – faith within the monetary system.

The next question I think we should ask ourselves is: *"Who is the head of the Church on Earth?"* Because the human Church needs a final word on opinion, conflict and debate. And that authority, I believe, is not through Intercession[1] or

---

[1] Prayer through proxy, usually a Saint.

the *"lost sheep of the house of Israel"* from Matthew 10:5-7. This is why it might be more appropriate to call Catholics, Marians. So their house is not a church, it becomes the House of Mary.

Fast forward a few hundred years to 1054, and a rift occurs between the Greek Orthodox east, and the Latin Catholic west. Why? On the surface, there appears to be a conflict over a piece of land in the Middle East. However, as incredible as it may sound, pending further investigation of the facts, I believe the East-West schism may have been because of the reluctance of Catholicism to include the New Testament in its doctrine. The question may not be why it has been slow to adapt but how to accept the truth that Christ's message was directed towards individuals may have hindered a better government. I say this because I believe Catholic intention might have been a universal effort begun under Ptolemy II in Egypt, continued with the Hellenists in Greece and later the Flavian emperors in Rome.

Christians should be careful in choosing between East or West since I believe one-world government will use all means at their disposal including dumbing-down populations until borders collapse and national sovereignty is replaced with a satellite form of technocratic authority appearing in every country and every land. If this sounds like a paranoid fantasy, then we should be aware that there are currently over two hundred central banks in the world and coincidence or not, most of them were established after the First World War and they all have one thing in common –

paper currencies. However, there is one that reigns supreme: the US dollar; sending and receiving in an electronic system of transfer and payment. Every transfer benefits the central bank of central banks founded on the eve of the First World War – the Federal Reserve.

How many faith-based institutions are telling their congregations they are continually losing their savings in a system of faith they have not even been made aware of? Anyone who preaches a conspiracy of subversive government agencies and their criminal behavior might find themselves on the wrong side of the law. Instead, they preach peace when there is an ongoing currency war between nations stealing from the very same congregations.

I believe Christians should not be legislators. No one should take the Law from the Jews. There should be no mistake about how wrong that would be for the choice between church and state we should be permitted to make. However, an individual who does not recognize a faith in Christ is an authority in the Spirit is a much more serious matter, no matter what side they are on.

So where does this leave Christians if they must argue in defense of Christ against his own mother? Should we teach there is a difference between churches and houses and then let everyone choose either the House of Mary or the Church of Christ? If you are Christian, the answer has to be there is only one Church guided by Christ based on an independent belief in the Spirit that does not compromise.

Unfortunately, as relates to law and government, the guidance of Mary when portrayed with a crown on her head may be considered a blasphemy or a heresy if Christ is made subordinate to the 'Mother Church', even if family is offered to a congregation as a legitimate solution to the struggle. However, since a family is formed through a legal contract – marriage, it is unfortunately not supported by New Testament Gospel. Quite the opposite in fact.

> *"For in the resurrection they neither marry, nor are given in marriage, but are as the angels of God in heaven."*
>
> Matthew 22:30[1]

I believe marriage should only be celebrated and supported by churches if matrimonial unions produce children. The law is not a spiritual union and families have specific legal rights. If Christians serve a purpose on this Earth, then despite my objections, we should accept Mary and government. I still argue we are not Christian without the Spirit. I believe it is impossible to teach Christian faith when Christ was a sacrifice or gave his life for better civic order.

We should not forget that even though Protestants would eventually challenge Catholic authority, they are all derivatives; bits and pieces of what preceded them, carefully selected or neglected in order to create something new and presumably better. In Europe and the west, it has been almost always from Catholic tradition, rarely if ever Orthodox.

I think it would be best to discuss Church authority. I would listen to any argument in scripture if it was part of a hierarchy. If an argument is based on source material from a higher level, I should have no better argument from any lower level; at least in theory.

However, this list does not include the highest authority; a part of the Trinity, and the body of Christ after resurrection. Its presence on Earth is the only substance I would call 'of the Spirit'. Since the Spirit is what makes Christianity spiritual and for the sake of my theory, I am of course talking primarily about metal since the immortal Spirit is the only thing a Christian should not question.

I have never heard of a Church preaching anything similar; that we believe in a monetary system because of a Christian faith in the Spirit; an eternal substance no human creates; that re-assures us of a continuous value from labor and is also an answer to the Struggle. Some people might be more likely to call such an institution a bank. If so, how Christian are banks? And how Christian are bankers? If faith is formed on the foundation of anything we believe in, should Christian belief be in any material substance? Does any substance we believe in make a faith worthy of being referred to as Christian? Because in the past unlike the present there is a long history of people having faith in a shiny metal even if today we are obligated to believe in paper, plastic or whatever comes next. Is our understanding of people hundreds of years ago that they were primitive and pagan and therefore less advanced than we are? No, their faith was a desire felt instinctively even if, before Christ, they had no answer.

If faith is an answer, then the future brings less assurance than the present or the past. However we honor, trust or give reverence we should not flatter anything or anyone with faith other than the eternal Spirit by implying the immortal exists to serve the mortal. It does not, and nothing of human creation or invention is superior or worthy of more faith than the Spirit and although we have sin, given to us from the past, that faith based system may not have been perfect but it offered salvation until it was taken away and no one objected on the grounds that it was criminal and anti-Christian to do so.

When I was young, I felt there was a less than subtle attempt to teach that money and human nature were the source of greed and materialism. So why would anyone try to make money Christian if it might be heretical to disagree? I believe the reason is judgment.

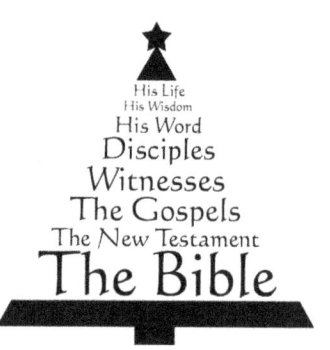

I think it is worth mentioning Matthew 6:9-13[1], and the optimism of King James in the year 1610 of a 'kingdom come'.

> "Our Father which art in heaven,
> Hallowed be thy name.
> Thy kingdom come,
> Thy will be done in earth, as it is in heaven.

> *Give us this day our daily bread.*
> *And forgive us our debts, as we forgive our debtors.*
> *And lead us not into temptation,*
> *but deliver us from evil:*
> *For thine is the kingdom,*
> *and the power, and the glory, for ever.*
> *Amen"*

It might not be an accident that bread has another meaning in common language – money. While we wait for a kingdom come we should remember how many have already been lost in time or battle because of bad faith and sin. If a kingdom come means the afterlife, death should not be a fast track to a heaven we desire on earth rather than in our grave.

Despite the implication that death might lead to an answer, I would say that since the time of Christ many have died without the truth and in defense of the indefensible so that in the world today, we were conditioned and made ready to live, as we are, to accept a blasphemy. I believe denying gold and silver and their authority over us, telling us there is an equal or better authority in currencies created by humans is a heresy. Something has replaced a long-standing faith in various metals, but not paper promises and certainly not faith in debt no one could possibly repay. If we must prove the Spirit in order to make the world a better place for all humans, let it be a currency or we will be judged for a sin that never gets forgiven because we have neglected a better moral order; better than law can give us. While I choose to conform, I wonder how many innocent lives also conform yet we all risk judgment just the same because of a sin that was committed on our behalf? And how worthy are we of salvation if we do not call it a sin and instead must bear witness to the inevitable suffering history says waits for us if we continue to defend ourselves with ignorance?

❧ THE PEOPLE vs. THE CROWN ☙

I have come to the conclusion that the reason for being indebted resides in the lack of a sense of morality. Individual debts are a moral obligation that limit the freedom of an individual, public debts are not. Democratic governments consider debt to be the will of the people while citizens do not recognize debt as their responsibility even when they derive a benefit from it. Debt and deficit have no moral effect on either. With nothing preventing them, they spend because they can. The absurdity is that when they overspend, their authority is often increased!

However, debt cannot be controlled if a vested interest does not exist to prevent a country becoming unprofitable to those who invest in labor. There is guilt in bankruptcy and there is shame in not repaying debts. One man's guilt should not be the burden of another and then become an ill effect on the broader economy. When it does, it raises the cost of living through inflation. The poor, mostly affected by the inflation tax, are kept ignorant of their condition when the government, supposedly acting in their favor, adds to it.

This is why I believe a long history exists of our effort to avoid judgment for our sins. Instead we have focused on our mortal being, working against a better order as we 'progressed' away from non-secular guidance and toward the idea of the poor being part of a better government. Whether it was a monarchy, a parliament or a democracy, we have rejected immortality in favor of what is human. The result is the fallacy that there is only mortal judgment.

Here is a timeline of Britain's path toward universal self-determination:

1126 - The Treasury
The approximate time of the foundation of the Monarch's store of valuables during the reign of King Henry I.

1279 - The Royal Mint
Coinage is consolidated within the walls of the Tower of London.

1429 - The Knights of the Shire
Parliamentary legislation establishes who is permitted to vote and lasts until the 19th century.

1688 - The 'Glorious Revolution'
When Catholic James II was ousted from power, Parliament took control of the mint from the Crown.

1694 - The Bank of England
A charter is purchased from the Crown with the seemingly impossible task of shaping public opinion of debt and private wealth into a sense of national unity.

1789 - A Revolution in France
The violent overthrow of monarchy is less important than creating a better system of credit and finance.

1803-1815 - The Banker's War
After Napoleon's defeat, Britain takes the lead as most credible lender.

1832 - Representation of the People
An Act expands voting rights in all boroughs across the United Kingdom to men above the age of 21 who are freeholders of property.

1833 - The Chancellor of the Exchequer
The Treasury becomes a ministerial department.

Thus began the development of the monetary system in England of common versus vested interest against the oft denigrated 'selfish' individual protecting personal wealth and property. The focus was on debt as a public service.

1867 - Expanded Reform Act
The category of eligible voters includes those with no property.

I sense a societal pressure put on the political spectrum in the 19th century to replace a role once reserved to the wealthy and charitable. Unfortunately, what is occasionally referred to by historians in the modern era as Christian Socialism, when successful, usually resulted in government spending more than it could collect.

1911 - The Lords Are Neutered
An Act of Parliament removes the right of veto on money bills from the Upper House.

1918 - Women's Suffrage
Parliament gives women a right to vote.

1946 - A Blank Cheque

For the benefit of social welfare programs, the Bank of England is nationalized.

1968 - Small Steps and Big Leaps

The Bank of England remains front and center in London's financial district while the Royal Mint is moved to Wales.

1998 - The Treasury Solicitor

The Bank of England is given a mandate to support the economic policies of the democratically elected government.

❧ A SELF-DETERMINED NATION ❦

Since I believe there is no greater fear democracy has than its people being apathetic enough not to vote, there must be some incentive to casting a vote. Although this timeline may appear slightly more political than financial, it should be noted that as voting rights became less centralized, so did banking became less private. Liberty, freedom and justice began very restrictive by today's standards, although somewhat liberal by standards still in force in Britain. Common characteristics of suffrage in the 17th and 18th century Colonies were male and usually included a property requirement of some value. A religious requirement was often included.

1660 - Plymouth Colony
Suffrage with a specified property qualification.

1665 - The Duke's Laws
New York restricts voting rights to landholders.

1671 - Plymouth Colony
Suffrage is further limited to freemen, *"orthodox in the fundamentals of religion"*.

1689 - Losing the Vote
Catholics are disenfranchised following the 'Glorious Revolution' in the UK; affecting Maryland, New York, Rhode Island, Carolina, and Virginia.

1776 - Independence
The former Colonies separate from Great Britain and become a self-governing republic – the United States.

1782 - The Bank of North America
Well capitalized with a large amount of gold and silver, it fails to meet government's needs yet still continues as a private bank for many years.

The newly formed government was a considerable credit risk until at least after 1790 when war debt was mostly settled at a considerable loss to the economy.

1789 - Distributed Responsibility
The US Constitution lets states decide voting rights.

1791 - The First Bank of the United States
Chartered and capitalized with mostly bonds, scrip[1] and an increase of taxes on whiskey, it fails due to land speculation and the Panic of 1797.

1807 - An Increased Risk of Default
The Act Prohibiting Importation of Slaves put financial pressure on Southern plantations.

1816 - The Second Bank of the United States
Chartered and capitalized with bullion from Europe.

---

[1] Paper currency issued by commercial interests with a third party guarantee, usually banknotes.

> *After President Jackson closes the Federal government's accounts with the Second Bank, it continues with a charter from the state of Pennsylvania. The ensuing crisis after 1840, particularly its effect on southern states, may have set the stage for the Civil War.*
>
> **1870 - The Federal Government Intervenes**
> A path to universal suffrage with the 15th amendment.
>
> **1920 - The 19th Amendment**
> Women get the vote.
>
> **1964 - The 24th Amendment**
> Voting by anyone who has failed to pay any tax.
>
> **1965 - The Voting Rights Act**
> The end of literacy and English language requirements.

I believe public control of the monetary system and spending in deficit meant a move away in the 1970s from military and wartime expenditure to more socially acceptable welfare and entitlement programs. People were less interested in the effort of uniting the world with faith and instead more focused on what economic benefit could be gained with a vote.

Now we have become so dependent on public welfare since the Treasury was looted and the keys pawned that even Daniel Webster[1] couldn't parlay them back without the majority finding the loss unacceptable.

---

[1] Legendary lawyer immortalized by writer Stephen Benét.

It is true that behavior cannot always be legislated and sometimes a law is ended when no longer relevant to the prosecution of certain crimes. However, if democracy is the slow path to moral decay when a majority of the people do not want to consider a greater purpose, is this because we fear a faith based system? If this is also true, then we have made a poor choice both figuratively and literally about a decision both legal and moral.

I'll end this chapter with an optimistic nod to the future from King James and Matthew 5:3[1].

> "Blessed are the poor in spirit: for theirs is the kingdom of heaven."

We should pray that those who struggle, although they are not aware of an answer, are one day guided less by secular institutions and instead by a faith in the presence of the Spirit.

the Eucharist

The Old Testament repeatedly warns against "sins of the flesh" – behaviors and desires that may feed the soul yet draw the Spirit away from God toward indulgence. Exodus 20:14 makes it clear that adultery (extra-marital relations) are forbidden, thereby sanctifying the institution of marriage. Other verses and chapters target specific types of adultery while Proverbs 6:32[2] sums them all up with:

> *"... a man who commits adultery has no sense; whoever does so destroys himself."*

The New Testament also contains explicit lists and condemnations of such carnal sins:

> *"Those who live according to the flesh have their minds set on what the flesh desires; but those who live in accordance with the Spirit have their minds set on what the Spirit desires. The mind governed by the flesh is death, but the mind governed by the Spirit is life and peace. The mind governed by the flesh is hostile to God; it does not submit to God's law, nor can it do so."*
>
> Romans 8:5-7[2]

> "But among you there must not be even a hint of sexual immorality, or of any kind of impurity, or of greed, because these are improper for God's holy people."
>
> Ephesians 5:3-5[2]

These verses reveal that carnal sin is not merely about physical acts. They are a rebellion against the judgment we find in the Crucifixion that I believe Christians should accept. We must remember a life centered on selfish desire, rather than on the Spirit has a broad effect on interpersonal relationships. Surprisingly, in marked contrast to the condemnation of carnal indulgence, Christ invites us at the Last Supper to partake of his flesh and blood. With his disciples, Jesus broke bread and shared wine, declaring:

> "While they were eating, Jesus took bread, and when he had given thanks, he broke it and gave it to his disciples, saying, "Take and eat; this is my body." Then he took a cup, and when he had given thanks, he gave it to them, saying, "Drink from it, all of you. This is my blood of the covenant, which is poured out for many for the forgiveness of sins."
>
> Matthew 26:26-28[2]

How should we understand bread and wine front and center in the Eucharist? Is this an esoteric mystery or a figurative ritual? The meaning is not rooted in satisfying physical hunger or any kind of carnal desire. Instead, bread and wine symbolize the guidance and sacrifice of Christ.

the Eucharist

Some critics have accused the Eucharist of being offensive, of eschewing Jewish tradition and Kosher law, even going so far as to claim the Eucharist is "cannibalistic". However, both the earliest Christians and Orthodox teaching have always rejected this literal interpretation. The Eucharist is a spiritual act, not a physical one. Early Church Fathers like Justin Martyr explained that the bread and wine are not ordinary food, but a spiritual connection through Christ.

This is echoed by Jesus himself in John 6:63[1]:

> *"It is the Spirit who gives life; the flesh profits nothing. The words that I speak to you are spirit, and they are life."*

The act of receiving the Eucharist is not a sin of the flesh, but an invitation to commune with each other, to be offered and accept the very essence of Christ himself.

Jesus' teaching in Matthew 4:4[1] crystallizes the spiritual nature of human existence and a deeper thirst or hunger:

> *"Man shall not live by bread alone, but by every word that comes from the mouth of God."*

Here, Christ draws from Deuteronomy 8:3, reminding us that physical sustenance is not enough for human life. Let's not think the Eucharist is about feeding the body, let it be the promise of the Resurrection. We should still use careful discernment and be aware of a moral consequence.

Paul cautions believers to approach the Eucharist with intelligent thought and introspection:

> *"Therefore whoever eats this bread or drinks the Lord's cup in a way unworthy of the Lord will be guilty of the body and the blood of the Lord. But let a man examine himself, and so let him eat of the bread and drink of the cup. For he who eats and drinks in an unworthy way eats and drinks judgment to himself if he doesn't discern the Lord's body."*
>
> 1 Corinthians 11:27-29[5]

Participation in the Eucharist is a call to holiness, not an excuse for immoral behavior. It does not save us from judgment if we blindly participate. It is a reminder that our actions – especially actions that flow from unchecked desire – might have adverse moral and spiritual consequences.

It is important to not reduce the broad spectrum of Christian faith only to ritual practice. While the Eucharist is a profound means of fellowship with Christ, it is not the sole measure of Christian identity or spiritual vitality.

In fact, there are reasons why not all Christians receive the Eucharist. Some Christian traditions understand the Eucharist differently, or celebrate it less frequently. Some believers are unable to receive due to uncertainty about its meaning or their own conscience. Despite this, they still have an assurance. The heart of Christian faith is not always in doctrine, but in faith of the resurrected Christ and the presence of the Holy Spirit.

Paul writes in Romans 8:11[5]:

> "But if the Spirit of him who raised up Jesus from the dead dwells in you, he who raised up Christ Jesus from the dead will also give life to your mortal bodies through his Spirit who dwells in you."

The proof of the Spirit in the Resurrection is the foundation of Christian transformation. Galatians 5:24[5] is the true sign of God's life within us.

> "Those who belong to Christ have crucified the flesh with its passions and lusts."

The Eucharist stands in stark contrast to Biblical condemnation of carnal sins, offering a spiritual feast that points beyond the flesh to union with Christ. While bread and wine are tangible, they remind us of many desires both physical and spiritual. They also remind us that the answer found in Christ is an answer to judgment that is not from Christ.

Because of this, the Christian life is not closed to those who for various reasons do not participate. Salvation is grounded in faith in the risen Lord and in the transforming power of the Holy Spirit. Christianity is a gift and a calling. The Eucharist is not an exclusive gateway to the kingdom of God; the ultimate proof of Christian faith is eternal life at work within us.

Freedom

I borrowed the title of this chapter from some source I cannot remember. The correct and complete quote is, *"Money is freedom in the form of a coin."* I find this appropriate because I believe money is a token of value based on faith.

> *"In all countries, however, men seem at last to have been determined by irresistible reasons to give the preference, for this employment, to metals above every other commodity. Metals can not only be kept with as little loss as any other commodity, scarce any thing being less perishable than they are, but they can likewise, without any loss, be divided into any number of parts, as by fusion those parts can easily be re-united again; a quality which no other equally durable commodities possess, and which, more than any other quality, renders them fit to be the instruments of commerce and circulation."*
>
> Adam Smith[1]
> *The Wealth of Nations*

Traditionally, money was not printed, it was minted. This was because it was metal. Not so long ago, in banking and finance, paper was synonymous with debt. Notes, contracts

---

[1] Highly regarded economist of free-market theory.

and loan agreements were all examples of financial obligation. Even notes backed by gold and silver were considered worthless if they could not be exchanged for the promises printed on them. Because if money was anything other than certain types of metal, it was open to deception and manipulation. The worst offense in any monetary system was currency conjured out of nothing with no guarantee of anything of value in its place. While lending and borrowing are not by definition, sinful, producing something that requires universal trust in what a human creates, despite anyone's best intentions, is a cheat and a fraud waiting to happen. Therefore, if we believe in money, knowing it is something eternally guided by Christ and the Spirit, we have confirmed faith and have established a higher moral order.

> *"Woe to you, blind guides, who say, 'Whoever swears by the temple, it is nothing; but whoever swears by the gold of the temple, he is obliged to perform it.' Fools and blind! For which is greater, the gold or the temple that sanctifies the gold?"*
>
> Matthew 23:16-17[2]

I avoid using the word money as much as I can since to me it represents something common and vulgar, something everyone takes for granted without considering it a part of a greater system of faith. Yet, whether it is metal, paper, plastic or digital, it only has a place in our mind as something of value and is therefore useful, even if we do not understand it as such, simply because of faith. We have faith in the bank that keeps it safe; faith in the value labor attaches to it; faith in some institution that loans, lends or invests. And, even though it may be abused by those in authority, over time we have learned to accept being guided by a currency based on credit. Someone might ask: *"Why do we tolerate not paying a debt? Why aren't we all fiscally responsible? Why not spend only what we have?"*

The simple reason debt is sinful is because it involves a risk made for profit. We are indebted when we borrow and when we borrow we are also obligated to repay. Until we do, we are in essence enslaved; working off the debt. Default means debt does not disappear, it becomes the burden of the lender who may pass on the obligation to repay to someone else. Yet because sin weighs so heavily in our mind as judgment held over us, we tolerate debt held by government thinking it no longer represents judgment. We find ourselves relieved not of the obligation to repay but of the responsibility to repay. We don't believe the debt the government has is our own. And likewise the government thinks the debt belongs to the people and has been created on their behalf. Is it a case of legislators forgetting that they are also citizens as well? Should we bother asking ourselves if a short-term benefit justifies a long-term risk if it involves the sin of denying the Spirit, a sin that never gets forgiven?

If we believe debt is a sin, we should be grateful to anyone keeping us from any self-righteous institution reminding us mere mortals of our tendency to commit acts that may not be forgiven, as long as we can manage debt without any adverse effect. Since most people today don't equate debt with sin, then how would they associate redemption with

Church authority? We have been conditioned to think that our guilt is not our own if we believe any presumed authority taught us that faith and freedom are in the law.

I believe that for currency to deserve faith it must maintain a value over time. In history, we have used any number of different material substances as currency and they don't all posses the same qualities or characteristics. We can theoretically use just about anything to represent a means of exchange. The question is should we?

In order to be a universally accepted currency, money must have a value attached to its substance. Payment to labor is the implied value. We should have faith in what money is made of not the fact we label it money. In order that we agree to the same faith, I believe unrestricted transfer and exchange is more likely when a list of characteristics includes:

> **Eternal** – In order that we avoid manipulation by any individual or institution, money should never be a man made material. The most devious individual or the most noble institution will, if given enough time, still tend to the same result: exploiting the system for their own benefit. This is why paper and plastic fail. Humans can create any amount at will while the substance will physically deteriorate over time leaving anyone who accepts it with nothing.
>
> **Limited** – This is not as obvious as it seems. If we had an unlimited quantity of anything, it would be so

common it would have no value. A significant part of gold's appeal is its rarity. Paper is obviously a wrong answer. I believe digital currency is a technological sleight-of-hand and just as liable to manipulation. We should know that the most advanced algorithms and encryption designed by the most well-meaning humans can be broken. The idea programmers are superior to elements only serve to flatter technocrats and those who employ them.

Tangible – This should be obvious. Currency must be portable. The most secure possession is one kept in your possession.

Durable – Currency must stand the test of time. Both in history and the human mind. This is why gold, silver, platinum and palladium all qualify. In fact, a long list of elements could qualify; some of which have been used as currency: aluminum, copper, gold, iron, lead, nickel, palladium, platinum, silver, titanium, tungsten, zinc. They are atomic elements that cannot be broken down into anything of any other substance we could make use of. Protons and neutrons cannot be held in our hands and therefore would not make good money.

However, in any argument in favor of precious metals, must be included recognition of their almost mythological reputation in popular culture as superlatives for quality and reliability; the finest, the best of the best, and so on ... The proletarian might criticize the capitalist who has it, and how they came to possess it. However, history has proved that neither would choose a lump of metal if paper has more authority.

Authoritative – Divine authority is more complicated than it sounds. Most people would assume that a number is applied to a coin. That would be correct. However, I believe denomination is not the solution, trust is. Say we use the historical examples of specie and bullion. If we accept that in the 1930s the United States moved the monetary system into public away from private and over to a bullion rather than a specie standard, then should we believe banks who were willing participants in that process had never been deserving of our trust? The Federal Reserve did issue paper denominated by a fixed value in bullion they held on our behalf. However, gradually over time, they printed more paper than they had represented in bullion.

Is it fair to say that banks are not trustworthy if they commit fraud? Common sense says yes, yet more than a few examples from history say no. Is it fair to say the government acts in the best interest of labor since the latter adds value to the currency of the former yet, to its own increased advantage, devalues the currency with the number of notes they print? Again, history says no, the silence of the majority seems to indicate either ignorance or complacency.

Since my theory rests on the premise that currency is a thing of faith, specifically the Christian faith, should perhaps another institution defend fixed denomination, forever honor the underlying substance of currency, in a spiritual sense? Manipulation could be avoided with public oversight, but deception would be impossible unless the Spirit is denied. If so, who would choose a separation of secular and non-secular where the State might be subordinate?

> **Appearance** – One final note, as relates to metal, is color. While not strictly speaking a requirement or as quantifiable as other characteristics, it may be worth mentioning that color, shade and luster are, according to preference, undeniably attractive, or not. Gold, 'the color of sunshine', glisters and gleams while silver, platinum and palladium are various degrees of cold and dull. It is worth mentioning a psychological effect since faith is often a metaphoric association. This is especially true when considering that with all the respect gold has, it is not the rarest of metals.

Some other questions we might ask ourselves include limiting use or controlling sources of production. Who should have this authority? Since I believe faith to be the foundation, who would support it and with what authority? We should consider that if we chose the Christian faith, it would be a blasphemy to deny and a heresy to offend the Spirit. How ironic that one day advanced civilizations in crisis might be afraid of a lesson from the past and a more superstitious way of thinking going forward. I also doubt there is anyone who believes in a judicial system, yet would agree to judgment in an ecclesiastical court.

I am reminded of his actions in the Temple.

> *Then Jesus went into the temple of God and drove out all those who bought and sold in the temple, and overturned the tables of the money changers and the seats of those who sold doves. And He said to them, "It is written, 'My house shall be called a house of prayer,' but you have made it a 'den of thieves.'"*
>
> Matthew 21:12-13[2]

And how they condemned him, perhaps not immediately, but eventually. Was this act of defiance his only offense? Or was it the proverbial straw that broke the camel's back? Who would have been most offended? For those answers, we should consider who allowed money changers into the Temple in the first place. I believe we are taught to blame Pharisees. They condemned Christ for the one thing they could not tolerate – criticism of what made them popular.

However, I believe any member of any party who has a position of power is unlikely to surrender to another authority without popular approval. How likely is that to happen if it involves a complicated understanding of faith and judgment and, in the case of the monetary system, the potential for a massive default?

Unfortunately, I believe accusations without accepting individual responsibility has proved the failure of generations of people to understand judgment as a fundamental and essential ingredient of Christian faith.

Maybe two thousand years ago, Jerusalem might have benefited from knowing that a monetary system guided by Christ and the Spirit could have avoided an inglorious destiny. A kingdom might have been in history, not scripture, a global empire and not become the tragedy of a failed Roman social experiment.

the Human Struggle

> "The greatest tragedy in mankind's entire history may be the hijacking of morality by religion."
>
> Arthur C. Clarke[1]

The Human Struggle or quite simply, the Struggle, is the colloquial name I give to our search for the answer to sin and temptation that we learn from Christ. I should be clear in saying that we don't find sin and temptation in Christ, we find an answer to the personal and social problems caused by human nature or more precisely human desire. We search for fulfillment in what is morally right and wrong while, at the same time, we are aware of the deception inherent in our conflict of what is moral and what is our nature.

I ask myself that if institutional religion has failed our moral compass, is there an answer in science? If literary fiction is an attempt to make science fact, then maybe, only if the greater failure is in our understanding that scripture is literary history and truth is supernatural philosophy.

---

[1] Popular writer of science fiction.

the Human Struggle

The problem with discussing the Struggle is the imposition of the more often misunderstood concept of sin and the idea that faith is in fact a barrier to freedom. I believe, when we are confronted with the potential for sin, we have an instinctive avoidance mechanism, when triggered within us, protects us by provoking feelings of guilt and shame. These

feelings aren't wrong, they are human nature. If sin is guilt after an offense is committed, then I believe shame precedes guilt with intrusive thoughts in our mind. What we might feel after certain types of behavior may never leave us. However, although shame can be a lesson learned, a sinful act, even if forgiven, cannot often not be undone. Therefore, when desire becomes a threat, even though only invoking shame in thought, we fear judgment.

I have to say the judgment we accept is human, the judgment we both fear and desire is not human. Eternal judgment is an authority greater than us that rules over our sense of right and wrong we should value more. Although there exists salvation, confession and redemption, how they apply to every sin is not easily understood in every human mind. However, I believe that unlike human judgment for social order, eternal judgment includes affection and approval. This means that eternal judgment is a moral direction between what we fear and what we desire.

Although the ideas of right and wrong vary among individuals, I don't believe a sense of right and wrong needs to be taught, unlike what is criminally right and wrong. Some concept of morality is inherent to all humans. We are all born mortal and moral and should learn that sin is a seductive powerful force and even though Christ could not resist, he was guided and protected by his faith.

☙ TEMPTATION ❧

'Then Jesus was led up by the Spirit into the wilderness to be tempted by the devil.'

Matthew 4:1[2]

It may be a mistake to call an offer from the devil temptation. It may be better to call it a seduction – an invitation to satisfy human desire. We should remember we all desire a great number of things and not all of them are sins. Thirst, sleep and hunger are good examples. Christ's forty days and forty nights without food and water would make anyone hallucinate. Thoughts would be reduced to the thinnest of reason. A rational mind in that situation might easily make a mistake and fall prey to their most basic instinct.

Christ must have known what to expect. If Christ was weakened when exposed to the elements yet, without food and water, his faith became stronger, his rejection of the devil's offers gave his ministry greater meaning. This is why I believe Christianity is an example of many things but most importantly, what I call the Struggle. I believe Christ was an answer to a problem that has plagued humanity since before the books of the Old Testament were written. The Struggle isn't disobedience of God. God gave us free will to choose. Yet, the Struggle is a source of sin. That must have been God's purpose in sending his only son. His life was proof of better judgment when we choose faith in the Resurrection.

❧ SIN ☙

> *"Who is he who overcomes the world, but he who believes that Jesus is the Son of God? This is he who came by water and blood, Jesus Christ; not with the water only, but with the water and the blood. It is the Spirit who testifies, because the Spirit is the truth. For there are three who testify: the Spirit, the water, and the blood; and the three agree as one."*
>
> 1 John 5:5-8[5]

Is it not generally accepted that Christ was without sin? If water is a force of nature and blood is both a symbol of life and of death then Christ demonstrates in Matthew 14:25 his ability to rise above temptation. And that is a useful talent to have should they become spoiled or tainted. However, let us remember that Christ was not a sacrifice, the blood in his veins was no better or worse than our own. His death is not our salvation either, even if his resurrection is proof of eternal life, it is also proof of eternal judgment.

Although Christ walked on the water of a lake, I'll use my example of water that moves anywhere. If a river to me represents a life force of nature that courses within us, then anything beyond the point at which it meets the sea, extends beyond a horizon and the limits of our understanding. Therefore, if nature is a source of sin and also our desire, I believe the only chance of salvation is a Spirit.

Of course Christ had to be aware of the source of sin. Christ was tempted in the wilderness with only angels to serve him. Yet his defense was to trust in the same Spirit that lead him to the wilderness. Trusting in the guidance of the Spirit may have been a greater challenge than arriving at a meeting with the devil. It could be argued that, leading Christ to evil, the Spirit was playing Devil's advocate. But the eternal Spirit knows that a human in the flesh, Christ the man Jesus included, had a God given human free will to make a choice. Christ's choice was to resist temptation, and live without sin, or Christ could not have fulfilled a purpose more so than any other prophet.

> *"You have heard that it was said to those of old, 'You shall not commit adultery.' But I say to you that whoever looks at a woman to lust for her has already committed adultery with her in his heart."*

Matthew 5:27-28[2]

Do we only believe what Christ is preaching because he himself is immune from any desire whether physical or emotional? Or do we believe him because he speaks the wisdom of his own experience? I believe the latter. A suggestion of this is when a woman is brought to him on a charge of adultery.

> *"He who is without sin among you, let him throw a stone at her first."*

John 8:7[2]

Christ knows what adultery means. In order that he knows, there must be a conflict in his mind. The law says adultery is wrong. He is therefore presented with an apparent contradiction in thought and behavior. In order to have faith he must believe he is without sin or does he think he is above the law? If not, is it only through a commandment he is able to recognize sin while also not offending the Spirit?

Why did Christ not cast a stone himself? Does Christ consider himself a sinner? The answer has to be that a lack of faith in a marriage is a legal issue. Christ's mistake would be making his faith a part of the law. That would impose his faith on government. Christ can neither condemn a sinner nor forgive them because of a greater judgment. If he did, he would instead reveal his own arrogance and conceit, and that would be an offense against nature, both human and of the Spirit.

Those who brought her to him were probably making every attempt to trap Christ with his own faith and thereby prove him no better than any other prophet. They probably left with only their hypocritical self-righteous indignation, choosing not to prosecute an adulteress only because Christ managed to turn justice against them. Will they not be satisfied unless Christ shows a disrespect of the law as well? Does the law prefer a conflict because the people who are its representatives do not respect themselves or their position?

Respect or not, I believe the law has no authority without the Spirit. It is not a blasphemy to deny Christ or the law, only the Spirit. If you are a Christian, you have no choice. Simply put, in order to be spiritual, we must choose faith in what is eternal and not mortal.

"The wild animals of the field will bless Me, the sirens and the daughters of sparrows, because I gave water in the wilderness and rivers in the waterless place, to give drink to My race, My chosen, My people whom I preserved to declare My virtues."

Isaiah 43:20-21[4]

We shouldn't think a man without sin is an abnormal human; cold and detached, bereft of passion or desire, even if we so often associate passion, desire, sin and temptation with physical intimacy, or as the Greeks referred to that difficult part of human nature, Eros. The paradox of faith is its symbiotic relationship with belief. They work together. Our knowledge of sin is based on the belief that with faith we are without sin. However, it would be unhealthy to repress human nature so, like Christ, we also struggle.

> *"For there are eunuchs who were born thus from their mother's womb, and there are eunuchs who were made eunuchs by men, and there are eunuchs who have made themselves eunuchs for the kingdom of heaven's sake. He who is able to accept it, let him accept it."*

Matthew 19:12[2]

God's judgment of mortal beings is whether we have faith or not. I believe that faith is in the Spirit.

Given that sin is immoral and affects the individual in a negative way, what should be done with sinners if their behavior has an adverse effect on those around them? It could spread from one person to another like a disease within a broader society. If crimes are punished, processed and incarcerated, yet sin is difficult to quantify, how do we protect ourselves?

This is why I believe when we are taught Christ's death is an atonement or forgiveness for sin, it is an over-simplification of a solution. Consider 2 Corinthians 5:21[2]:

> *"For He made Him who knew no sin to be sin for us, that we might become the righteousness of God in Him."*

Was Paul teaching that Christ was sin?! We could not believe in Christ as a better example of ourselves if he possessed any sin whatsoever. I find it offensive when someone suggests he was a sacrifice. I do not think it possible someone could die for sins committed by another person, unless they die because of the sins someone else has committed. I think many people believe they are being taught their sins are excused because of the crucifixion. That is, if they learn what is in the Gospel, sin will have no adverse effect on their life. Do someone think memorizing scripture makes them immune from evil? We cannot possibly believe that. When a sin occurs, the only solution is confession. If we don't confess we don't recognize a mistake has been made. I believe only through confession and recognition of sin, Christians have the possibility of salvation and redemption.

the Human Struggle

❧ THE MARRIAGE CONTRACT ❧

The best place to begin a discussion on marriage within the context of monetary theory is not from scripture, it is with a publication by Anglican priest and economist Thomas Malthus who in 1798 wrote *An Essay on the Principle of Population*. Malthus' reason for population growth is an increase in the food supply. Presumably, fluctuations in either will affect the other until the population can only be checked with some upper limit ending in famine or too many people.

> "I do not know that any writer has supposed that on this earth man will ultimately be able to live without food. But Mr. Godwin* has conjectured that the passion between the sexes may in time be extinguished. ... But towards the extinction of the passion between the sexes, no progress whatever has hitherto been made."

Malthus speaks of virtue and perfection. If the answer is in believing that an increased population creates misery and vice, wouldn't it be a benefit to promote abstinence? Hasn't that always been a policy of the church? Apparently not. Here is a quote:

> "When the mind has been awakened into activity by the passions, and the wants of the body, intellectual wants arise; and the desire for knowledge, and the impatience under ignorance, form a new and important class of excitements. Every part of nature seems particularly calculated to furnish stimulants to mental exertion of this kind, and to offer inexhaustible food for the most unremitted inquiry. Our mortal Bard says of Cleopatra:

---

* See Index.

> *Custom cannot stale*
> *Her infinite variety.*

> *The expression, when applied to any one object, may be considered as a poetical amplification, but it is accurately true when applied to nature. Infinite variety seems, indeed, eminently her characteristic feature. The shades that are here and there blended in the picture give spirit, life, and the prominence to her exuberant beauties, and those roughnesses and inequalities, those inferior parts that support the superior, though they sometimes offend the fastidious microscopic eye of short-sighted man, contribute to the symmetry, grace, and fair proportion of the whole."*

The context of the quote from Shakespeare's *Antony and Cleopatra* Act II, Scene I is here included simply because of its reference to a religion.

> *"Age cannot wither her, nor custom stale*
> *Her infinite variety: other women cloy*
> *The appetites they feed: but she makes hungry*
> *Where most she satisfies; for vilest things*
> *Become themselves in her: that the holy priests*
> *Bless her when she is riggish."*

Shakespeare's use of the word riggish means sexually active. Apparently the Queen of the Nile was a bit promiscuous and her behavior was condoned by members of her religious establishment. Although Egypt was not a Christian nation, one would think that an Anglican priest would not even mention this in the sense of nature, which as Malthus goes on to say is the nature of the world around us.

I assume this includes the birds and bees? The idea clashes in my mind of artistic vision and a much more idealized depiction of nature. Implying these uncontrollable passions require a defeatist attitude rather than a considered understanding of sin and a spiritual understanding, might make Malthus a priest of some other religion promoting 'the vilest things'.

Had Malthus forgotten the wedding in Cana in John 2:1-12[2] when Christ turned water into wine, not because he wanted to, only because of the insistence of his mother? Were Christ's words, *"Woman, why do you involve me?"* and *"My hour has not yet come."* disrespectful? Was Christ uncertain about marriage and the persistent threat of sin? If sin is present even in marriage, then was Christ willing to compromise only out of respect for his own biological family?

I am surprised Malthus chose Shakespeare instead of anything Biblical. Not that I would either. The reason I would choose any other source for matters concerning human temptation is the severe lack of authority in Christ's words or behavior. He may have had wisdom. Did he have knowledge? What of a few examples in Matthew 19:9, 19:12 & 19:30 confirm how we make up our own mind about Christ's answer to his own struggle? Which of the confused disciples scratching their heads and shrugging their shoulders said in Matthew 19:10[1]: *"If such is the case of the man with his wife, it is better not to marry."*

On the other hand, if the Church promotes non-marital relations, the advantage might be an increase in the number of a congregation? Since there has been an inverse relationship in the last few hundred years between population growth and church attendance, I don't believe an increase in the human population has meant more Christians on Earth.

> "The advocate of the perfectibility of man, and of society, retorts on the defender of establishments a more than equal contempt. He brands him as the slave of the most miserable and narrow prejudices; or as the defender of the abuses of civil society only because he profits from them."

If population growth and the human struggle are both related, and the solution is Christian, then any attempt made by a non-secular institution should first hide its association or face the contempt and scorn of presumably libertarians?

I was quite surprised that Malthus could not argue that population be kept in check through education and things 'virtuous and perfect'. I assume the reason is in the unspoken teaching of some denominations of Christian churches that teach happiness is a large family and that marriage is a fulfillment of God's purpose on Earth and an answer to sin. I believe this to be Malthus' intention, although never stated clearly, because he is very critical of Parish law particularly as relates to the poor. If the Church is failing to serve the poor, then what does a member of the Church think about government and social welfare?

Malthus says Poor Laws help no one since they prevent the misery that keeps population in check and create an environment where rich and poor compete for a limited resource. Although he seems against faith based welfare, Malthus does offer a solution.

> *"To remove the wants of the lower classes of society is indeed an arduous task. The truth is that the pressure of distress on this part of a community is an evil so deeply seated that no human ingenuity can reach it. Were I to propose a palliative, and palliatives are all the nature of the case will admit, it should be, in the first place, the total abolition of all the present parish laws."*

Odd that an ordained priest preaches against what often involved the charitable role of a church in those communities and instead preaches anti-capitalist rhetoric and government intervention.

> *"Secondly, premiums might be given for turning up fresh land, and it possible encouragements held out to agriculture above manufactures, and to tillage above grazing. Every endeavour should be used to weaken and destroy all those institutions relating to corporations, apprenticeships, etc., which cause the labours of agriculture to be worse paid than the labours of trade and manufactures."*

> *"Lastly, for cases of extreme distress, county workhouses might be established, supported by rates upon the whole kingdom, and free for persons of all counties, and indeed of all nations."*

And then there is this: *"But the farmers and capitalists are growing rich from the real cheapness of labour."*

That may not be true. A book by 20th century author Garet Garrett called *The Devil's Bushel*, although it was a fictional narrative, presents the idea that overproduction of a resource like wheat lowers the price at market for the producers whether or not the profit in trading futures or options is greater or less. Farmers in the novel grow more and quicker to be the first to market and gain the best price. The solution developed by one of the characters is to introduce a crop disease into a harvest in order to increase the profit to farmers.

The main character in the book, whose instinct has always been to win, tries to lose a fortune. However, because he works against common sense, he beats the competition and actually gains more than he loses. The message here must be that the market won't respect the unknown forces of nature, human or otherwise. It won't judge intention or motive. It might respond to whoever has the greater amount of capital. Garrett was highly critical of FDR[1] and the New Deal so it is simple enough to conclude that the biggest player in any similar free market game would eventually tip the balance of uncertain nature in their favor with unlimited cash.

As controversial as were the decisions FDR made, were they immoral in the sense that a better supply of food benefits social order? In the 18th century, overpopulation may not have been the threat we are aware of today; of a growing human population that would displace other species of plants and animals while polluting the air, land, rivers and

---

[1] Franklin Delano Roosevelt; US President during the Great Depression.

oceans with everything humans consume and waste. We became more concerned with survival than the effect our decisions have on eternal judgment.

The reality is large multi-national corporations and government subsidies guiding food production, along with genetically modified seed growing about ten times more from every hectare of equivalent land in Malthus' day. Indoor cultivation has just about removed nature from the equation making food available year round in all climates and weather. The result: a debt and credit based system that has increased the human population from approximately one billion people in 1800 to 7.5 in 2025!

the Eternal Spirit

Were there Christians before a child was born in Bethlehem? If so, what were their beliefs and in what did they place their faith?

> *'Then Moses returned to the Lord and said, "I pray, O Lord, these people have committed a great sin and have made for themselves a god of gold."'*
>
> Exodus 32:31[4]

Well, that certainly answers what people might choose to believe if given a choice. Disregarding the commandments himself, Moses breaks the tablets given to him by God and then orders a mass murder. If that wasn't bad enough, he makes the Israelites drink the ground up dust of the golden calf. As insane as this all sounds, it's almost comical.

This story only has any sense when it's boiled down to human nature. What is worthy of reverence, we honor. And we accept what has value according to our instinct. Were they told "*no gods before me*" a little too late? Unfortunately, commandments weren't enough to make them obey. They gravitated instinctively toward more primitive behavior. However, does that mean there was no better faith until Christ?

Christ comes from the Greek word Christos and is a title translated as 'anointed'. Christ was someone blessed or gifted with wisdom. Using the title in its proper order, Christ Jesus frees us from the uncertainty of human existence. What Christ taught initially was referred to as 'the *Way*'. I discuss in a separate chapter that his life was an answer to the '*Struggle*' and how we understand sin.

The synoptic gospels are in agreement the Spirit cannot be denied even if denial of Christ is not a sin.

> *"Therefore I say to you, every sin and blasphemy will be forgiven men, but the blasphemy against the Spirit will not be forgiven men."*
>
> Matthew 12:31[2]

> *"Assuredly, I say to you, all sins will be forgiven the sons of men, and whatever blasphemies they may utter; but he who blasphemes against the Holy Spirit never has forgiveness, but is subject to eternal condemnation."*
>
> Mark 3:28-29[2]

> *"And anyone who speaks a word against the Son of Man, it will be forgiven him; but to him who blasphemes against the Holy Spirit, it will not be forgiven."*
>
> Luke 12:10[2]

Notice that the Spirit is placed in a position of greater respect than Christ himself. It doesn't surprise me the book of John doesn't make mention of the Spirit since the word faith is so rarely, if ever, found in many of its translations. However, John does mention the source of faith.

> "It is the Spirit who gives life; the flesh profits nothing."

John 6:63[2]

I believe blasphemy or slander might also include denial. Ignorance of the Spirit may invoke pity if on a path of enlightenment but denial means the forgiving God of the New Testament will not forgive, because asking for forgiveness from someone whose existence you deny is absurd.

I won't give a complete history of religion before Christ. If such a thing were possible, it would almost certainly be incomplete. What I believe is essential to understanding any religion is asking ourselves: Is it literature or is it historical fact? Is there proof of anything or anyone in scripture? What I would say is: "Does it matter?"

We are the highest minded beings on Earth, and when put together, have always been using our time and our minds looking for answers. And although we have come a long way, we still have many unanswered questions. Some are related to science, biology, psychology or other fields of interest. I believe a great many are related to faith.

When discussing faith, no matter where or when we have ever existed, I believe the source of the answers to those questions may have come from the same place in every human: temptation and desire. From the chaotic disorder in trying to understand thoughts, feelings, and make sense of our own existence within our mind, came order and language.

We generally believe truth is fact and made up stories are fiction. Whether true or not, we still choose what we believe. If a capacity to sin is part of our nature, we have nothing else to guide us in the Struggle without faith.

Fortunately, so long did we pray for an answer to our passion we were given the idea of a Christ; that he was fully conceived in heaven and delivered. The physical embodiment of an answer that by the grace of God, became a mortal being. Grace I would say was not sacrifice. I would define his life as an answer in eternal being. So, when we choose to believe in what is not mortal, it is because of scripture.

Let me add this random bit of trivia: The Stater was the official currency of the Lydian empire issued during the reign of King Alyattes (619-560 BC). Generally considered the first coin authorized by a government, it was so much more. It was an alloy of gold and silver called electrum. And it, like any monetary system, required faith. A monetary system that, six hundred years later, in the time of Christ, was still in its infancy. Now, 2,600 years later, the monetary system still hasn't matured! Is this because of a lack faith? Or is it because we choose not to believe without proof?

What are the differences in the relationship between faith and belief? Can one exist without the other? We should all know we can believe anything including, through trickery and repetition, things we have been conditioned to believe. We can freely choose to believe lies or the truth, or be unaware we are conforming to subconscious systems of positive and negative re-enforcement.

So what about proof? Does faith need proof? Gravity doesn't need faith. It is so consistent, it is considered a fact and is included in the category of science which claims to only represent facts. Yet, a scientist may choose not to tell you no one knows how gravity works.

> "When I was a child, I spoke as a child, I understood as a child, I thought as a child; but when I became a man, I put away childish things."
>
> 1 Corinthians 13:11[2]

Christ's message taught to a child isn't science. It appears more philosophical since it depends heavily on what we think and cannot be measured: everything infinite and eternal. An intelligent being and a creator before our own, and after, that has no beginning and no end. Does the human mind have the capacity to understand an infinite universe? Yet, without a human mind, there is be no concept of time, essential for understanding a beginning and an end.

So that presents a contradiction; like the proverbial chicken or egg. Which comes first, belief or faith? And why waste any effort if, when brought into this world, we accept what we are told without question? There would be no individuality.

> "Don't waste it, because it doesn't grow on trees."

I laugh when I think back to what I received every week in my allowance. It was advice and paper. And I should have reminded my dad that he, a paper mill engineer, worked at a company that made paper for bank notes! Why I might have doubted his advice is because at the time we were living in a small town, surrounded by hundreds of square miles of thick forest, punctuated only with an occasional mountain, lake or river. Of course I know now that he would receive no salary, and his family no benefit, unless they were cut down and processed.

> "The woods are lonely, dark, and deep and I have miles to go before I sleep."

Anyone familiar with this poem[1], should know I have deliberately misquoted it. I would repeat this line to myself when I was young because the woods were lonely, not because of a lack of people but because of a lack of faith. I believe eternal faith is found in our sense of being alone.

Those cold canyons of commerce and industry are a source of an existential crisis because they lack what we desire.

---

[1] Robert Frost, *Stopping by Woods on a Snowy Evening*.

the Eternal Spirit

Pedestrians, shoppers and office workers may seem to offer human comfort but the streets are empty without a common faith to unite us. Concrete, brick and mortar do not satisfy human desire and from the point of view of nature represent only a dishonorable waste, that if humans were to suddenly no longer exist, nature would have to find a way to process all the material we have exploited for our own benefit in order to return the earth to the state it was before our creation – without the plants and animals we have made extinct. And yet, in the last few centuries, we have blindly pursued a policy of increased consumption and population growth. Faith in nature can only condescend to those brought up without better guidance in such an environment.

I was taught at a young age that proof of God's existence is in nature and what has been created by God, best illustrated in another poem[1]:

> *"All things bright and beautiful,*
> *All creatures great and small,*
> *All things wise and wonderful:*
> *The Lord God made them all."*

So familiar to so many, this left me conflicted with who God was, until I considered the relationship of the creator of heaven and Earth and the being in charge of the forces of nature; of the life force and energy that sustain us. Nature perhaps is less important and should Earth end may no longer exist even if we believe in a single greater infinite being.

[1] Cecil F. Alexander, *All Things Bright and Beautiful*.

Occasionally, I find it necessary to remind people that Easter is not Christian. According to English monk and Saint Bede, Estre was the pagan goddess of spring. At least we are keeping her memory alive with the Resurrection while others may continue to celebrate Passover.

Do we risk being labeled pagans if we believe in an infinite masculine and an infinite feminine and both cycles of birth and death? What if we ask ourselves how we were conceived, why we are here and an answer is not found in the Bible? Assuming God even created nature and 'all things well', then the only flaw in our lives as humans 'in his image' is our own lack of faith, in creation and ourselves. A faith that is only understood by a relationship between human nature and the nature of the world around us.

However, proving eternal life has its problems. And that problem is doubt. Doubt we have about what we choose to believe in could cause faith to fail. I don't look for an answer to what I should believe in, I am like the Christians before Jesus who when he arrived and spoke must have recognized the possibility of the answer to a need they already had and to a few it must have been a light illuminating the darkness. Although it might have confirmed what they already believed, I am sure they must have had their doubts.

I discuss in another chapter my thoughts on the Eucharist. I would prefer eternal life not in the bread and wine, the body and blood of anyone. I would prefer to put my faith in something substantial, tangible, worthy of worship, respect, and reverence. And most important of all, something that has a power and authority to guide us because our faith is not in anything human.

In this day and age, I have the advantage of history. I can look back and see what has proved itself time and time again. Were the early Christians looking forward to a day of electricity, the internal combustion engine or transistor radios? I don't think so. What they should have looked forward to was a world made better with faith. I ask myself, if given a choice, would more Christians choose a ritual centered around bread and wine or shiny metal?

Metals are a real substance on Earth. I can pick them up and hold them. I can carry them. I can give and receive this faith to other people who believe like me, they have an additional value because our governments share that faith, even at the risk of money being more deserving of praise than the law. However, if anyone accepts what I am saying, do they also accept a Christian faith?

❧ AGAPE ☙

Given that a substance is worthy of faith, what makes that substance better when it is made the solid foundation of a monetary system? Besides knowing what we hold in our hand is the very definition of the Trinity and therefore judgment. Only through faith are they brought together becoming the fusion of the spiritual and physical making possible the relationship of all people with God. Isn't that the very definition of Agape?

Of course, if we require proof in order to believe something and if that is the only path to faith rather than believing institutional religion, then all we have is doubt unless, like Reverend Whately in his highly influential 19th century book *Christian Evidences*, we put all miracles and mysteries into a category labeled 'Supernatural'. In doing so, we risk teaching children that cheap and popular entertainment in movies and comics have the answer when their superheros all appear to fight for law and justice.

I know combining the monetary system with Scripture creates a potential complication if we say it is also an answer to the Struggle. However, if we must have an answer that satisfies the individual before we are able to construct a better system of faith, then my theory is the antithesis of what might only be constructed on behalf of society if a majority has to deny human desire.

ಹಿ THE HUMAN CHARACTER ೞ

Since spirit and spiritual are often used loosely to mean many things, I have developed a more precise, less theological approach to the Struggle. I included an illustration on page 125, for the most part based on introductory concepts in human psychology. Chart 8.1 is a visual representation of how I believe characters relate.

Character is based on three ingredients: gender, orientation and gender identity. Although gender is simply a biological male or female, gender identity is a little more complicated since it doesn't always follow assumptions made about an individual's perception of their physical self. I believe gender identity is fixed at birth. However, environmental conditioning in our upbringing or the nature of physical attraction may make it appear much more fluid. While gender and identity can be understood at a young age, because the third ingredient, orientation, relies on being an adult, it cannot be fully understood before adolescence.

There are three main groups of individuals: Paternal, Fraternal and Filial. Each group possesses a primary and a secondary character. I will admit that determining character is not always accurate. I am not sure if it is a useful skill that can be easily learned. However, after so many years of practice, I occasionally find exceptions I can't explain. So use at your own risk. No warranties or guarantees are implied. ☺

8.1 Human Character

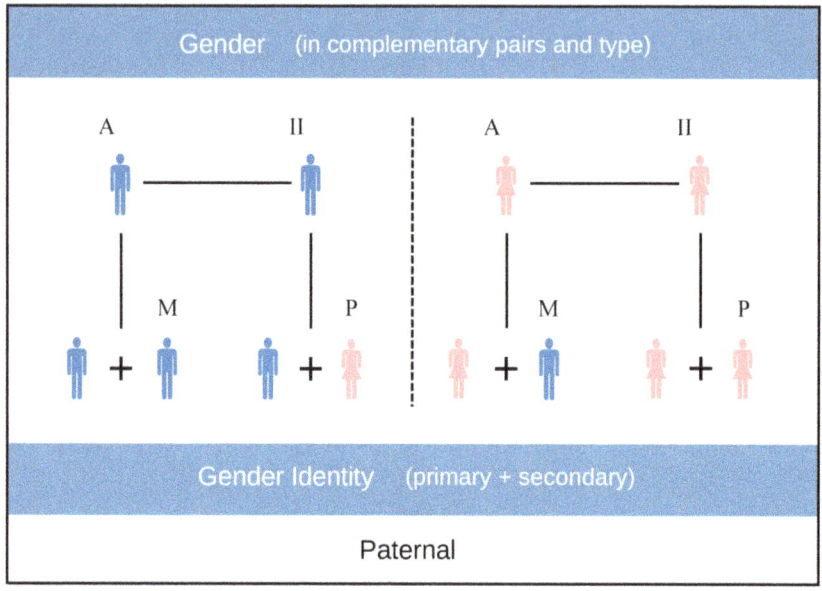

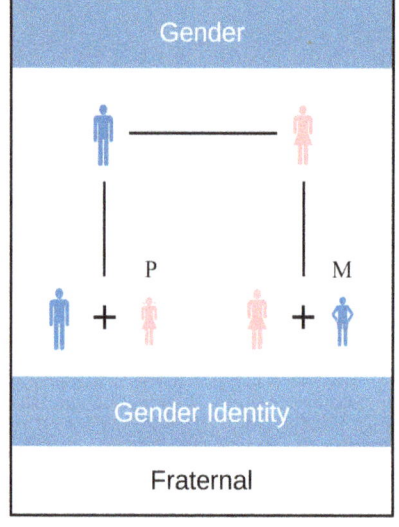

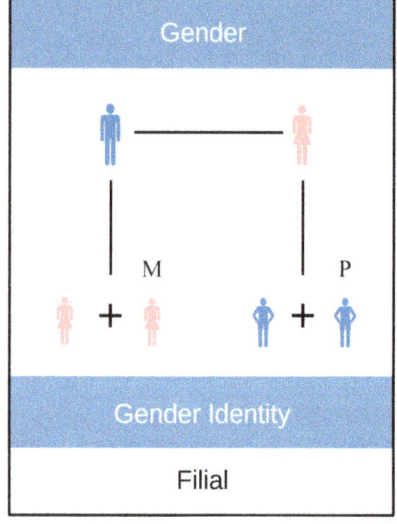

Mature male   Mature female   Immature male   Immature female

Here are a few observations I have made:

- Paternal characters are always mature. Filial characters are always immature.

- Primaries relate to primaries and secondaries to secondaries. They never 'cross over'.

- Physical unions are ideal if characters compliment one another. That is to say, a filial married to a fraternal or a paternal would not be ideal. Note that within the paternal category there are separate male and female groups and they are not ideally compatible.

- A spiritual relationship involves complimentary secondary characters; one being P, patriarchal and the other M, matriarchal.

- The paternal category is subdivided into male and female since complimentary pairs are always formed with the same gender.

- A & II are personality types very loosely defined as dominant and passive.

- Some character types might be easily mistaken for another. An example is paternal type II and its similarity to female fraternal. The difference is the secondary of a type II is mature, the fraternal is immature.

- Unlike primary characters, secondary characters only form spiritual relationships with an opposite gender identity. I have never noticed an exception.

I believe each of the separate identities – primary and secondary, perform different roles. Primary characters are responsible for what is conscious and physical. Secondary characters respond to the subconscious, the emotional and therefore I believe are the source of what is spiritual. Secondary characters establish relationships with other beings based not on physical gender, relationships are based on gender identity.

At this point, I hesitated to include a conversation about orientation. I believe many of us are reluctant to discuss Christ's personal life to such an extent. Unfortunately, since my theory is centered around the idea of sin and that the source of sin is human desire, I would offer no better interpretation of scripture than anyone who believes a thirty-something bachelor had a better answer to the Struggle if we don't include an understanding of character; character that I believe in every human is defined in some part with orientation.

"Don't ask and don't tell." was a popular slogan in the 1990s related to orientation in the US military. I believe Christians should consider asking themselves difficult questions like, *"Who does, who doesn't, and why?"*

I could argue Christ's orientation one way or the other. I find nothing that confirms any specific leaning. Maybe deliberately ambiguous was the purpose of those who transcribed his life, making his story more accessible to a greater number of people, even if risking serious questions related to the Struggle.

However, there are reasons I believe Christ is a valuable source of wisdom when discussing judgment and sin. The first is that he was wholly conceived in heaven and delivered to a mortal woman for a mortal life. The second, that he was without sin and although suffered human judgment, he was given favorable judgment by a greater power; proof of which is the Resurrection. The third may be the most controversial: Christ must have been the answer to human desire.

> *"Who is he who overcomes the world, but he who believes that Jesus is the Son of God? This is he who came by water and blood, Jesus Christ; not with the water only, but with the water and the blood. It is the Spirit who testifies, because the Spirit is the truth. For there are three who testify: the Spirit, the water, and the blood; and the three agree as one."*

1 John 5:5-8[5]

I believe this trinity is more in line with the Struggle in blood (death), water (desire) and the Spirit (judgment).

> *"And being in anguish, he prayed more earnestly, and his sweat was like drops of blood falling to the ground."*

Luke 22:44[3]

I consider the garden of Gethsemane account in Matthew 26:36-46 a controversial part of the Gospel. Jesus was condemned, betrayed and sentenced to death. For what? While I detect a strong sense of the Struggle, it would be hypocritical to say that any particular act involving sin is wrong and some other similar act is acceptable if we believe Christ had some random answer for his. For that reason, I believe Christ was not sent to die for our sins unless they include more than temporal thought. Even if we fall victim to a desire, we have to accept we may not receive favorable judgment or eternal life. Yet, there are some of us who believe we are saved because unlike Christ, our desire is not the same as his.

Paul says, in so many words, money is the root of many kinds of evil. I recommend reading other epistles not written by Paul while giving thought to the Struggle. Should we accept that any act to satisfy human desire might be a blasphemy and a sin if not guided by the Spirit? We must not be spiteful or arrogant and wage war against ourselves or a better faith that might unite us all if we fail to recognize sin in ourselves or forgetting grace, we congregate simply because we create exceptions to our recognition of sin.

I know I criticize the superficial and the esoteric in certain institutions and secret societies. I know I risk being labeled a hypocrite if I preach blind faith. But what divine knowledge do we already seek in psychology, sociology or some other academic discipline that may not include Christ's message or imply the Spirit is some ethereal luminescence and teach that the answer to the Struggle is physical, human or anything secular?

Whether any truth is scientific or Gospel, we need to believe in something. The reason is morality. Even if someone's

Johannes

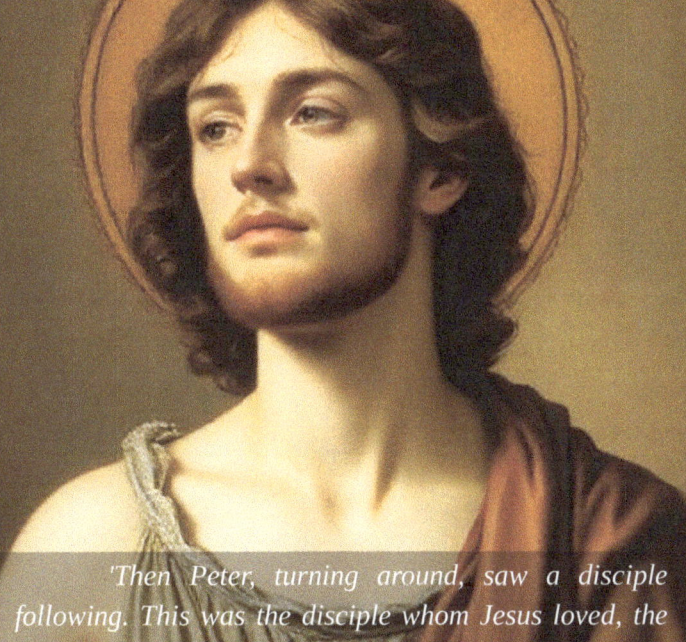

'Then Peter, turning around, saw a disciple following. This was the disciple whom Jesus loved, the one who had also leaned on Jesus' chest at the supper and asked, "Lord, who is going to betray you?" Peter, seeing him, said to Jesus, "Lord, what about this man?"

Jesus said to him, "If I desire that he stay until I come, what is that to you? You follow me." This saying therefore went out among the brothers that this disciple wouldn't die. Yet Jesus didn't say to him that he wouldn't die, but, "If I desire that he stay until I come, what is that to you?"

John 20:21-23[5]

ability to reason is equal to our own, we question their judgment. Creating the idea of an independent Spirit on Earth in order to justify our own tolerance of bias, whether an individual or a nation, I believe gives a sense of fair judgment to any system or institution that creates social order.

We may have been wrong about the monetary system because gold and silver have been denied and we were never taught what our parents believed in because, like their parents, and grandparents I believe they were not taught a better faith that to them was a part of their instinct and nature. They were taught to believe in the superiority of what is human. A power was given to a blasphemy because Christ died trying to deliver us from the evil we fall prey to if we choose to believe any mortal being, even his, rather than being united in a Spirit.

> 'Then the Pharisees went and plotted how they might entangle Him in His talk. And they sent to Him their disciples with the Herodians, saying, "Teacher, we know that You are true, and teach the way of God in truth; nor do You care about anyone, for You do not regard the person of men. Tell us, therefore, what do You think? Is it lawful to pay taxes to Caesar, or not?"
>
> But Jesus perceived their wickedness, and said, "Why do you test Me, you hypocrites? Show Me the tax money."
>
> So they brought Him a denarius[1].
>
> And He said to them, "Whose image and inscription is this?"
>
> They said to Him, "Caesar's."

---

[1] Coin of the Roman empire.

And He said to them, "Render therefore to Caesar the things that are Caesar's, and to God the things that are God's."

When they had heard these words, they marveled, and left Him and went their way.'

Matthew 22:15-22[2]

Notice there are two parts to his answer – give what has authority from Caesar, back to Caesar and pay your taxes. Since a denarius was made of silver, give recognition to what belongs to God. Although the coin may have been 'legal tender', the substance only had any greater authority because humans could not create it. Even after being mined, minted and denominated by humans, an element is still the result of an intelligent design from a greater mind than our own.

The Pharisees were pleased with Christ's indirect support for their party and their worship of money. The Herodians, who depended heavily on the benefit bestowed on them by the taxpayers, would certainly agree to people paying more to government. We might not know that coins had been issued by Judea's ruling monarch. What a trick that was to have him choose between Caesar and Herod and instead Christ chooses an immortal element.

They were all exposed as vain and self-serving if they believed Christ's answer flattered them. Even if they laughed at Luke 23:6-12 and Christ's humiliation when they dressed him like a king and sent him back to be judged. Did they mistakenly believe Christ justified power held over people who consider themselves blessed when they are compensated with a token of the only source of value in an economy back then as it is now? If that is money, flattery probably wasn't what Christ intended when he called the center of social order in Jerusalem a 'den of thieves'.

So, we have established that the monetary system in Christ's day was a faith based system; faith in a head of state on a coin and faith in what a coin was made of. If we accept that this is also a spiritual exchange, then the only question we should ask ourselves is, "*Are we making the same mistake today, or is it worse than it was in Jerusalem when anyone attempts to unite the world with a system of exchange using paper or anything man-made?*"

the Intercession of Mary

> "From now on all generations will call me blessed, for the Mighty One has done great things for me – holy is his name."
>
> Luke 1:48-49[3]

In case it isn't obvious, this chapter's title refers to Biblical Mary and some of England's earliest monarchs who weren't kings. They were in fact some of the first queens to rule in their own right. Since this chapter overlaps both the chapter on the Human Struggle and the Body Politic, rather than incorporate into either, I decided to make a separate chapter on its own.

I believe we should maintain a male preference in the human kingdom given the example of the genetic disposition in most of the animal kingdom. I also believe a bias toward male best represents the intention of male authors of scripture toward a male audience of the usefulness to a kingdom of lessons in scripture. However, since males aren't always available, is it possible to substitute a female instead?

the Intercession of Mary

Although it was not known at that time, science has since informed us the male carries the genetic code that decides gender. And that may or may not matter. My theory only asks if we should accept that if left with no male heir and only a female do we apply different rules with a female monarch than with a male? If we accept there are two crowns – one for a queen, another for a king, then neither should wear one meant for the other.

"Near the tomb of Mary and Elizabeth remember before God all those who divided at the Reformation by different convictions laid down their lives for Christ and conscience sake."

Tile on the floor
of Westminster Abbey

I believe the problem with the 16th century Reformation in England under Henry VIII was not defending independence of any sovereign land from foreign influence, it was the acceptance of female succession at the end of Catholic rule and the purpose of Christendom.

The Succession to the Crown Act of 1543 and Henry's will after his death in 1547, attempted to iron out the details of succession among his many wives. While it did effectively eliminate the need for an armed conflict to settle next in line to the throne, the glaring omission in my mind is an issue brought up by the Scottish throne under Mary Queen of Scots and the Crown-matrimonial – a husband's right to rule in place of his wife.

the Intercession of Mary

I believe, although rarely mentioned was an issue, the Scottish Queen may have been in favor of such an idea, whether or not some say it was because of her husband. Although not discussed to a great extent, the matter of male preference was at least settled with her death. The Act only stipulated that the three Queens: Mary, Elizabeth and Jane should seek the Privy council's approval before any matrimonial union.

While much has been written about the Reformation, I only draw attention to the reign of Mary I and her half-sister Elizabeth. I am deliberately ignoring the epithet placed on the former's reign and her title 'Bloody Mary'. I don't accuse or excuse anyone. Christ's church should be matters related to the human struggle and the Spirit. Other judgments are best left to secular courts.

When Mary was made Queen, through determined effort on her behalf, she had to fight against the previous monarch, Edward VI and his decision to leave the Crown to someone else. Not married when Edward died, and she became Queen in 1553, Mary clearly stated her intention and the result of her success:

> "For I am already married to this commonwealth, and the faithful members of the same, the spousal ring whereof I have on my finger; which never hitherto was nor hereafter shall be left off. Protesting unto you nothing more acceptable to my heart, nor more answerable to my will, than your advancement in wealth and welfare, with the furtherance of God's glory."

Of course that was not enough for a nation that was used to Catholics as rulers, just not if they were female. Raised primarily by her mother, Mary had the benefit of a complete method of education created on her behalf. Even if she had been taught to be an independent minded woman, the pressure was on producing an heir to the throne. When it was announced that Mary might wed a Spaniard, a rebellion was led by Thomas Wyatt who with many thousand men assembled and marched on London. Unafraid of the rebellion, Mary was not sure of Wyatt's intention and gave a speech at Guildhall in the City of London. Although it was transcribed, I believe the speech was hastily prepared or not at all. Even if it might have been misheard, because of what it contains, it should be regarded as historically relevant.

It is not clear why Wyatt and his men were against the idea of the Queen's marriage to a Spaniard or anyone else. However, I think this speech contains a better reason for a rebellion:

> "I am come in mine own person to tell you what you already see and know; I mean the traitorous and seditious assembling of the Kentish rebels against us and you. Their pretense (as they say) is to resist a marriage between us and the prince of Spain; of all of their plots and evil-contrived articles you have been informed. Since then, our council have resorted to the rebels, demanding the cause of their continued emprise. By their answers, the marriage is found to be the least of their quarrel; for, swerving from their former demands, they now arrogantly require the governance of our person, the keeping of our town, and the placing of our councilors. What I am, loving subjects, ye right well know – your queen, to whom, at my coronation, ye promised allegiance and obedience. I

was then wedded to the realm, and to the laws of the same, the spousal ring whereof I wear here on my finger, and it never has and never shall be left off. That I am the rightful and true inheritor of the English crown I not only take all of Christendom to witness, but also your acts of Parliament confirming the same. My father (as ye all know) possessed the same regal estate; to him ye were always loving subjects. Therefore I doubt not, ye will show yourselves so to me, his daughter; not suffering any rebel, especially so presumptuous a one as this Wyatt, to usurp the government of our person.

And this I say on the word of a prince. I cannot tell how naturally a mother loveth her children, for I never had any; but if subjects may be loved as a mother doth her child, then assure yourselves that I, your sovereign lady and queen, do as earnestly love and favor you. I cannot but think that you love me in return; and thus, bound in concord, we shall be able, I doubt not, to give these rebels a speedy overthrow.

Now, concerning my intended marriage; I am neither so desirous of wedding, nor so precisely wedded to my will, that I needs must have a husband. Hitherto I have lived a virgin, and I doubt not, with God's grace, to live so still. But if, as my ancestors have done, it might please God that I should leave you a successor to be your governor, I trust you would rejoice thereat; also, I know it would be to your comfort. Yet, if I thought this marriage would endanger any of you, my loving subjects, or the royal estate of this English realm, I would never consent thereto, or marry while I loved. On the word of a queen I assure you, that if the marriage appear not before the high court of parliament, the nobility, and commons for the singular benefit of the whole realm, then I will abstain – not only from this, but from every other.

Wherefore, good subjects, pluck up your hearts! Like true men, stand fast with your lawful sovereign against these rebels, and fear them not – for I do not, I assure you. I leave with you my lord

> *Howard and my lord treasurer [Paulet], to assist my lord mayor [Myddelton] in the safeguard of the city from spoil and sack, which is the only aim of the rebellious crew."*

Mary clearly states that if it is the will of the people, she will marry and produce an heir, if not, then she won't. This is something we all consider a personal matter, don't we? Although she prefers to not marry, she is giving herself over to what is best for her country. I argue that such a decision should not have been a matter of law or tradition. It was honor. Let's not forget, Mary's mother had to face public humiliation in order to defend hers against her own husband.

Unfortunately, Mary's offer of dedicating her life to her people meant no support for what she might have preferred, instead it meant her sacrifice. Was her request as a queen to be treated like a common farm animal in need of stud services?

History says Wyatt failed and was executed. I wonder what might have happened if he had received a copy of Mary's speech before arriving in London. And where was the Archbishop of London? Was Bonner too busy executing heretics (allegedly) that he couldn't attend to a serious threat involving a Queen's honor?

Be that as it may, history also tells us Mary went ahead with a marriage and after a few miscarriages, produced no heir and died at a relatively young age. Apparently marriage to a country and to a man wasn't avoided on the grounds it would have been polygamy. I would only add that if she had chose not to be wed, she may have been remembered as wedded to the Church instead.

What is odd is her half-sister's reign. Elizabeth I took up the cause for whatever reason and copied most of Mary's character and became known as the virgin queen married to her country! Why did she so closely resemble the monarch Mary might have been if she had survived? Was it a lack of confidence in her ability to lead? If gender were the issue, we could argue that men represented a significant percent of the members of the court and the Privy council, but even so, Elizabeth didn't appear to resist male advice. Not that she would, unless they were members of a gender-biased Church which apparently must have been part and parcel of a conspiracy. In a letter to five Catholic bishops she writes:

> "Was it not you and such like advisers that... stirred up our Sister against us and other of her subjects?"

Showing what a well-versed political leader she would become, Elizabeth attempted to blame the same bishops for the Reformation.

> "As for our Father being drawn away from the Supremacy of Rome by schismatical and heretical counsels and advisers, who, we pray advised him more or flattered him than you, good Mr. Father, when you were Bishop of Rochester?"

Was historical inaccuracy an indication of weakness in forming an argument from her own opinion? Or was it a noble act of defiance she could carry forward? If she were acting in defense of Mary, I could just as easily act in her defense and say Elizabeth was wrong, English bishops were put to death for their opposition to the king and the Reformation. Perhaps she was conflicted with how to be patriarchal and, I sense, an anger directed toward her father? Examples suggesting such do exist. I wonder if a husband might have tamed that shrew?

> "We give you, therefore, warning, that for the future, we hear no more of this kind, lest you provoke us to execute those penalties enacted for the punishing of our resisters, which out of our clemency we have foreborne."

So she ends the letter with an ultimatum: 'Discuss the truth and put your lives at risk.'; later developing a habit for ending arguments with threats and occasionally following through with them. She was so uncertain of critical decision making that when she signed a death warrant for Mary, Queen of Scots, she had the man who carried out the order arrested and put in the Tower of London because she said not to execute it! That is the kind of mixed-message authority one should avoid. If taking responsibility for one's actions made Mary a tyrant, then historical revision has made the Elizabethan era a wonderful time of flourishing arts and entertainment when the roots of a great empire took hold only because of the greatest queen England ever had.

Adding insult to injury, after her death, Mary's request to be buried next to her mother was ignored. If faith didn't improve either of their lives, government compromise cursed one of them when they placed Elizabeth next to her.

When I look at their history through letters and speeches, I detect two distinctly different women. One who appears very self-sufficient and another who leans heavily on other people and threats to maintain their authority. Even if this is a very crude way of forming a psychological profile, I believe each of us whether male or female are defined differently as matriarchal or patriarchal.

If Mary was known as 'precocious' when young and we define precocious as mature in one's years, then I believe Mary's relationship with her mother might have made her the former. However, Elizabeth's inability at a certain age to recognize her own bed chamber and an alleged 'embrace' by a member of the court that led to her exile when added to a possibly conflicted relationship with her father makes her appear to be the latter. If they were of different character types, then Mary would have the confidence to rule on her own conscience (dare we say faith?). If patriarchal, I believe Elizabeth might have done better to have married and produce an heir. However, these very different women could have done better for everyone if they had focused primarily on what was best for themselves.

So what of 'conscience' chiseled into the stone at the foot of their final resting place? If conscience means what is morally right and wrong then what can be concluded from a

Roman and a Church of England Catholic[1] when through one there is not the Intercession of Mary and in the other there are only solitary thoughts? How sad is the situation when someone cannot find intercession in their prayer? How absurd is a church service if, because of denial of the Spirit, there are pious members praying for guidance yet only receiving final word on faith from a secular source?

---

[1] There exists a 'High' Church of England believing itself Catholic and only seperated from Rome.

Doubt

> "Now after Jesus was born in Bethlehem of Judea in the days of Herod the king, behold, wise men from the East came to Jerusalem, saying, 'Where is He who has been born King of the Jews? For we have seen His star in the East and have come to worship Him.'"
>
> Matthew 2:1-2[2]

I had just recently completed reading *Easy Lessons on Money Matters*; a long out of print book from 1853 by the Reverend Richard Whately when I re-wrote this chapter. The title intrigued me so I gave it a shot. Although it was aimed at students as young as eight years old, it was somewhat scant of depth even for that age. To be fair, it might have appeared much more grown up to children back then. I decided to include it in a discussion since it reminded me of my own experience over a century after its publication of my youthful effort in trying to understand the purpose of a Christian message albeit without any Church or school making a direct reference to the economy or money. The book however was mostly optimistic in its approach but left me questioning its utility to an impressionable mind given the author's lack of the undeniably corrosive effect of inflation on wages.

> "When a poor man has saved up a little money, he generally puts it into the Funds (as it is called), or deposits it in a Savings Bank, which does this for him; he is then one of the Government-Creditors, and receives his share of the taxes. You see, therefore, that if the National Debt were abolished by law, without payment, many, even of the labouring classes, would lose their all; and the English nation would not be relieved of the burden; since it would be only robbing one set of Englishmen for the benefit of another set."

The implication labor must purchase government debt since higher taxes would make us all worse off is not good advice. Inflation is the promise of theft of savings from too much debt in circulation! The idea of higher taxes should make us argue against the need for more debt. The book held many other naive and convoluted explanations of different concepts but I was left wondering if what we refer to as Christian might be the fault of our current predicament if not many previous as well. Perhaps being an archbishop, Whately was all too aware that labor strife might lead to social unrest and students of any classroom may be sons and daughters of government ministers. I discovered in another source he was very concerned with a curriculum of instruction teaching both Catholics and Protestants alike. Doctrinal differences aside, from the perspective of any modern-day 'establishment', teaching Christian economics and a monetary system where saving is best and debt is bad might be considered at best a fringe effort and at worse antagonistic. In fact the most resistant to accept such archaic ideas might be those who have already been taught that any improvement might lead to a conflict. So we wait until it breaks, then fix it? We have the situation now that if the economy were a vehicle we rode around in, it would be more repairs than actual vehicle.

However, politics may have played an inconspicuous and greater part in Whately's writing. Given what we have today, the Church and faith-based institutions give less in relief and charity than the government in welfare and entitlement programs. This shift in roles is one of the reasons why we have wealth redistribution. Taxation replaced voluntary contributions making the church less relevant particularly in its most useful capacity in education.

Other than that, I agree with a lot of what Reverend Whately wrote, even though I was quite surprised he did write something so uncharacteristic of organized Christian religion; and that meant speaking openly and favorably about human instinct.

> "... a bank-note is not really money, but a promise to pay money. No one would give anything for a bank-note, if he did not believe that any one would pay gold or silver for it."

> "It is not, therefore, labour that makes things valuable, but their being valuable that makes them worth labouring for."

He does make a distinction between 'busy-work' which may keep workers happily employed and the motivation of profit from capital investment in businesses employing those same idle workers. In doing so, Whately may have inadvertently expressed a bias for private rather than public employment.

> "Most of the money that is spent, however, is laid out in employing labourers on some work that is profitable; that is, in doing something which brings back more than is spent on it, and thus goes to increase the whole wealth of the country."

> "The more capital there is in a country, the better for the labourers; for the poorer the master is, the fewer labourers he can afford to employ, and the less sure he can be of being able to pay them."

> "It is curious to observe, how, through the wise and beneficent arrangement of Providence, men thus do the greatest service to the public, when they are thinking of nothing but their own gain."

> "... every man should be left free to dispose of his own property, his own time, and strength, and skill, in whatever way he himself may think fit, provided he does no wrong to his neighbors."

His statement about political economy, which was a somewhat recent invention at the time, is quite surprising. It might have been unfair to criticize since it had not yet become ingrained into the establishment and it seems more likely a warning about cartels and labor unions.

> "It has been shown in a former Lesson that all attempts of Governments to regulate by law the rate of wages are useless and mischievous. Indeed it may be said that more harm than good is likely to be done, by almost any interference of Government with men's money transactions, whether letting and hiring, or buying and selling of any kind."

A summary of Whately's philosophy has to be that common sense will prevail until workers moving from an agrarian to an industrialized society demand a government that will make their life better. Which the former did with organized labor, and the latter didn't with the monetary system.

The perception I have developed from looking back at the last few hundred years is, generally speaking, lessons in scripture tell us that Christ and Christianity are in some way against money and wealth. Anyone who isn't of a similar mindset, especially the wealthy, must suffer wrath and scorn on par with their self-centered attitude. If they don't instead prefer legal consensus, they are not good Christians or at the very least should carry the greatest burden of guilt.

Perhaps this is true with a debt based fiat[1] system but I don't believe the same about a system based on metal. The message of Christ's faith is an applied system of exchange and value that answers the human struggle with a better faith. Faith empowers labor with a secure and stable compensation. Faith is already a monetary system that exists, whether we are aware of it or not, only because the paper currency we choose to believe in, unlike the Spirit, has value.

However, I would argue that in order to deserve being referred to as Christian, money must not be faith in what is mortal, it must be faith in what is eternal. This is why when Christ taught faith in the Spirit, and we apply that belief to a

---

[1] Latin word meaning 'let it be', used in this context to mean paper currency.

currency, it is no longer what is commonly referred to as money, it is intelligent design and should be recognized as its presence on Earth.

In order to oppose the bias and prejudice of those who say different about the Christian faith and the monetary system, here are some examples of what I believe are misquoted or misunderstood passages from scripture I consider have not been interpreted correctly.

❧ GOD & MAMMON ☙

> "No one can serve two masters; for either he will hate the one and love the other, or else he will be loyal to the one and despise the other. You cannot serve God and mammon."
>
> Matthew 6:24[2]

Although commonly taught as synonymous with money, I believe Mammon may have been a deity equivalent to Plutus, the Greek god of wealth, and the Roman equivalent, Saturn. Students of history should know that Saturnalia, the festival of Saturn, merged with the northern European tradition of Yuletide to create the Christmas holiday we have today.

Despite being a deity, the word mammon[1] was antithetical in the sense that if wealth is material gain, it takes away from faith. Some depictions of Plutus with other goddesses Eirene and Tyche, appear oddly similar to art and sculpture of the infant Jesus and Mary. If the quote from scripture is correct within a monotheistic view of creation, the implication is no one should attempt to combine both material with spiritual. However, if we include Eve's deception in Genesis 3:22[5], do we have a better understanding of human conception and other 'gods'?

> 'Yahweh God said, "Behold, the man has become like one of us, knowing good and evil..."'

---

[1] In some translations of scripture, mammon is used in place of money.

Doubt

I believe knowing good and evil is accepting both light and darkness. They set limits and boundaries that define one another. We exist in a universe of both. We posses some amount in our nature. That is to say, we were brought into the world innocent and yet susceptible to evil we recognize when we find it in our being human. We may have disobeyed the will of God and fell from grace, yet it is with the Spirit we are saved. If we understand heaven on earth because of the essential ingredient of an eternal Spirit, perhaps God and Mammon can also be combined and made useful to us through a common faith.

In Rome, early Christians built Churches on top of temples to the mystic sect of Mithras. Why? Was it an attempt to replace an archaic and profane use of cult behavior? If so, then why were similar cults created later if Christianity was a more refined construct of an already venerated god that also offered salvation and redemption?

Could it be said the followers of Mithras had something in common with the esoteric rituals of other highly influential secret societies? As hollow and harmless as they may may seem, style and fashion appear to have made Christianity appear less practical and useful to each successive generation. Although I know very little about the people who worshiped Mammon, I will trust in history and offer Christ's resurrection and the Spirit as the development of a better system of faith.

Doubt

> *Thomas said to Him, "Lord, we do not know where You are going, and how can we know the way?" Jesus said to him, "I am the way, the truth, and the life. No one comes to the Father except through Me."*
>
> John 14:5-6[2]

The Spirit's presence in some immortal substance like an atomic element becomes a constant reminder of the threat of darkness, the promise of light in wisdom and a purpose in our mortal being guided by a Spirit.

Believing in the independence of the Spirit from the Trinity, its presence on Earth and in heaven, is essential to understanding why currency is faith. If the relationship within the Trinity is held together by a spiritual union then it is quite possible to refer to currency as possessing what the Greeks called Agape – a spiritual connection with the Creator, through which we all relate. Unfortunately, in its presence and superior design, we are made humble and reminded of our own judgment and tendency for sin.

🔊 THE EYE OF THE NEEDLE 🔊

> *"And again I say to you, it is easier for a camel to go through the eye of a needle than for a rich man to enter the kingdom of God."*
>
> Matthew 19:24[2]

Before I comment on this, I should mention that the *"eye of the needle"* refers to a narrow passage in the wall of Jerusalem left open day and night while all other gates were closed. It was narrow in order to more easily guard it. So, Christ is implying the City of God, Heaven or Jerusalem does not accept anyone with any amount of material wealth, only spiritual wealth, or faith.

Yet, it is so often interpreted to mean the wealthy are not welcome in the afterlife. Nonsense. I believe Christ meant to say that no one can purchase their way into a future kingdom of heaven, if one should exist in Judea or anywhere else. The power money has to humans on earth has none in a kingdom founded on faith. Because in heaven, access is granted for the devout, whose faith in the Spirit, sets aside a place for them.

As it relates to material wealth, a passage rarely mentioned is the rich man at the crucifixion who in Matthew 27:57-60, offered to place Christ's body in his own recently constructed tomb. Even if he was a materially blessed convert, it was the Pharisees who requested it be sealed for three days to test the prophecy of Christ's resurrection.

The point I am making is irony. It took wealth, those who worshiped money and a substantial amount of doubt in order to prove true wealth is knowledge and faith. On the other hand, The Resurrection made possible with the Spirit both delivered and saved Christ with the benefit of material wealth. To us, this is the proverbial 'leap of faith' made impossible if we do not recognize the mistake in Jerusalem wasn't to condemn our mortal being, it was to deny the Spirit.

❧ THE ROOT OF EVIL ❦

This last example is probably the most commonly misquoted and various translations say it slightly different.

> *"For the love of money is a root of all kinds of evil, for which some have strayed from the faith in their greediness, and pierced themselves through with many sorrows."*
>
> 1 Timothy 6:10[2]

I imagine this classic line has ended innumerable discussions promoting faith in currency because it appears to make money synonymous with evil. How more anti-Christian could anything else be? I believe this complicates things a bit, because if we accept what Paul is saying then it would appear I am committing a heresy since I believe the monetary system is based on faith. If is based on faith in the Spirit, it becomes a blasphemy since I have associated evil with the presence of the Spirit.

> *"O Timothy! Guard what was committed to your trust, avoiding the profane and idle babblings and contradictions of what is falsely called knowledge — by professing it some have strayed concerning the faith."*
>
> 1 Timothy 6:20-21[2]

Unless Paul is playing devil's advocate, should economists await judgment for being false prophets if preach something different?

Doubt

I have heard it said, although I am not sure how true it is, that a symptom of demonic possession is slander; defaming someone through words. So, if we question why a Pharisee would make such a statement, we should look perhaps at what may have possessed him. Paul wrote to Timothy when he was in Rome, required (some say *requested*) at an audience with Nero[1] on charges of an offense against the state religion. The letters to Timothy are the last words we have of Paul. Many historians consider while in Rome, he died a Christian martyr. So is it a safe assumption to believe he was mentally and physically exhausted, fearing punishment for charges brought against him? Like Christ at the crucifixion, did this provoke in him a final expression of doubt?

> Now from the sixth hour until the ninth hour there was darkness over all the land. And about the ninth hour Jesus cried out with a loud voice, saying, "Eli, Eli, lama sabachthani?" that is, "My God, My God, why have You forsaken Me?"
>
> Matthew 27:45-46[2]

Was Paul, in Acts 23:6[2] attempting to blame his fear of judgment on being a true believer?

> But when Paul perceived that one part were Sadducees and the other Pharisees, he cried out in the council, "Men and brethren, I am a Pharisee, the son of a Pharisee; concerning the hope and resurrection of the dead I am being judged!"

---

[1] (b.37-68) Roman emperor.

Paul, a past and current member of the party of money worshipers, apparently feels no remorse or guilt. Why would he? He uses his membership as his best defense against judgment, not with God, with the support of other Pharisees. And then Paul the hypocrite condemns his own people when, like a bad Pharisee, says in no uncertain terms money is, "the root of *many kinds of* evil." And we know that statement is slander, and therefore a sin, when we believe Christ teaches we give and receive only because of faith through the Spirit and the Creator with one another.

Perhaps we should forgive Paul, he was under a lot of stress. Like the stress he was under, also in Acts, when he claimed to be a Jew so he would be treated fairly and not charged as a criminal by the Sanhedrin. And then he claimed to be a Roman citizen so as to impress a centurion and avoid being flogged.

This puts us in a difficult position. If we believe the monetary system is based on faith, we must forgive the earliest and most well known evangelist of a surprisingly dissimilar conclusion.

Alchemy

> "Science can teach us, and I think our own hearts can teach us, no longer to look round for imaginary supports, no longer to invent allies in the sky, but rather to look to our own efforts here below to make this world a fit place to live in, instead of the sort of place that the churches in all these centuries have made it."
>
> Bertrand Russell[1]
> *Why I Am Not a Christian* (1927)

Alchemy is simply an archaic word of what today we call chemistry. Its effort in Medieval times was mostly focused on using crude methods to manipulate different substances, turning one into the other. An early attempt to understand and control the forces of nature only known to the creator. It could be said the reason for our effort was the insatiable curiosity for knowledge although, as relates to certain metals, especially our feeble attempt to turn lead into gold, was obviously for profit. Unfortunately, those attempts failed. Perhaps only because we used lead.

However, despite what you may have heard, alchemists have made huge leaps forward.

---

[1] British philosopher and Nobel laureate.

Alchemy

My research finds that experimentation in the 1920s by Hantaro Nagaoka at Tokyo Imperial University claimed to have turned mercury into gold; small amounts were  supposedly produced from electrical vapor lamps. This was later confirmed by Adolf Miethe in Berlin Technical High School but has not been confirmed by anyone since. Confirmation is apparently inhibited by the cost related to research. We should not give up on our best effort though. The discovery of cold fusion in 1989 seems to enable the transmutation of certain metals. In theory, particle acceleration may produce the same result.

So, there does not appear to be an obvious threat to a better monetary system. Humans could not produce more precious metal than had been placed on earth in the first place and therefore no detrimental effect to a fixed value in circulation based on limited quantity. At least, not at present. However, human ingenuity being what it is, a process may be refined and become much more cost effective. It should be noted that, *'the probability of anything increases with what is possibile when given enough time'*.

We should remember the example of aluminum, now the most common of metals, so rare in the 19th century, it challenged silver for its prominent position until men by the

Alchemy

name of Héroult and Hall found a way to improve production. Look at its role in manufacturing and construction today.

Unlike other metals, brought down from up on high, no longer fit to be a currency because they were either too common or too costly to produce. But time marches on and so does a theatrical song and dance promoting one metal over another. Although we excluded gold and silver, most in the US are made from copper, nickel or zinc. While central banks still choose to store gold, patiently waiting in the wings are platinum and palladium, unless digital currencies decide to steal the show.

So what about the medieval science of alchemy today? While science continues its effort to understand these building blocks of matter in the universe, have advancements in research served us better than faith in the Spirit? I believe Fascists and Zionists created a conflict in order to remove a better store of value and a medium of exchange only because of its threat; a threat my theory refers to as eternal judgment. An application of the Christian faith we were never taught was rejected in favor of the system we have today, a faith in paper and human judgment.

I believe Christian and Science are two words which should never be put together. Faith is not a science. We should understand when we study scripture, we are able to apply philosophy in some useful way. I think a mistake was made after the Atomic age when the effort to understand the monetary system in some concrete sense meant a move away from philosophy, most evident in institutions of higher learning, toward mathematics, giving the appearance of secular truth to theory.

Since 1969, when the first Noble prize in economics was awarded, the emphasis has been on '*models of economic processes*', '*analysis in economic science*' and '*structure*'. With the development of award, compensation and recognition, institutions of higher learning have been encouraged to teach a scientific and not a philosophical approach. Among all the pie and bar charts are calculations based on formulas and algorithms few lay people could understand. You would need as many years in academia and as many degrees framed on the wall to even make an attempt. It's disguise is quite indulgent and elitist. Yet this academic trend and its influence on government is undeniable.

It should be no surprise my theory is critical of this approach. It should however be a surprise if I suggest that a more appropriate category for what I believe is the faith-based branch of economics: the monetary system. If I am right, then it appears we have strayed too far in the opposite direction.

A quick search on the internet reveals a website with one hundred economists throughout history from ancient Greece to the present day, with their schools of thought, their theories and contributions. However, a keyword search on the site returns absolutely nothing when I type in Christ, spirit or faith! Why?

The most well recorded historical reference to a Christian monetary system has to be the Knights Templar from the 12th century. They were arrested, excommunicated and burned at the stake in 1314 by French king Philip IV who was heavily indebted to them for amounts presumably he could or would not pay. It was relatively easy to repudiate debts owed to any other faith and the Jews were more than willing to forget earlier ill treatment and resume positions in banking and finance even after forced appropriations and expulsions. But not so with the Templars. They had been highly regarded in early international banking in what today might be called cross-border exchanges and settlements for pilgrims going to the Holy Lands. Given Pope Clement V's decision during the Avignon Papacy might have been sympathy for his childhood friend the king, the shocking sentencing and execution can only be considered an example being made by Philip for an intolerance of authority being placed over the monarchy.

That said, France did however establish a tradition of international credit and banking that lasted until the Revolution in 1789. Unfortunately, if history is a precedent, we should look no further than the Knights for an example of what any government will tolerate. We may have learned a valuable lesson in combining the domains of Church and State.

Alchemy

In the last two thousand years since Christ we have been on a self-serving path and solely focused on our own mortality. Perhaps Galileo[1] and his *Dialogue* in 1632 was an affront to Catholicism. If that was so, then how do they classify the crowning achievement of a branch of science known as physics when it makes a mockery of doctrine and names a plan for mass destruction the Trinity Project?

> *'And Jesus answered and said to them: "Take heed that no one deceives you. For many will come in My name, saying, 'I am the Christ,' and will deceive many."'*
>
> Matthew 24:4-5[2]

Governments on all sides employed physicists who assaulted for political gain those building blocks of matter which are atomic elements, whose elaborate design and structure was once only known to the Creator yet is how I believe a better monetary system is established.

> *"Then they will deliver you up to tribulation and kill you, and you will be hated by all nations for My name's sake. And then many will be offended, will betray one another, and will hate one another. Then many false prophets will rise up and deceive many."*
>
> Matthew 24:9-11[2]

Could it have been that Galileo wasn't being Christ-centric in his research? If he had, he might have avoided the wrath and scorn of the Vatican. So, where were the critics during the Manhattan Project? Were they made calm and

---

[1] (b.1564-1652) Controversial Italian astronomer who supported Copernican heliocentrism, the idea the Earth revolves around the Sun.

reassured, or in a world going mad, were they too terrified to say anything?

If so, was developing an atomic bomb the only sane option? Why was lead physicist Enrico Fermi[1] never called to answer for his actions? Would another Inquisition[2] not have been a wise decision? Atomic research must have been kept in such air-tight secrecy until Hiroshima and Nagasaki that scientists could defend themselves from a hysterical mob with the idea it was really about safe and affordable electric power for an entire city of the future. Although the Vatican has since stated an objection to nuclear weapons, they appear to support the use of nuclear power for energy production. When considering the Spirit's future relevance, it is still a dangerous compromise.

> "But there were also false prophets among the people, even as there will be false teachers among you, who will secretly bring in destructive heresies, even denying the Lord who bought them, and bring on themselves swift destruction."
>
> 2 Peter 2:1²

What promise is faith with peace? How can Christians defend the Spirit if they are made to fear war and only serve government? If faith creates a conflict, then it is only uncertainty about what we choose to believe and why.

If so, then we are in opposition to ourselves in our own mind until we are in conflict with one another and war might

---

[1] Italian physicist and designer of the first Atomic bomb.
[2] Catholic courts of inquiry.

mean we have peace when we rest in peace. Therefore, if faith is not in a Spirit, there may be a final war destroying all of creation. Unless of course, no wars have been about faith. Then we are the nihilist architects of our own chaotic destruction and we die as we lived – without reason. Like Nostradamus[1], Christ has this to say in Matthew 24:23-25[2]:

> "Then if anyone says to you, 'Look, here is the Christ!' or 'There!' do not believe it. For false christs and false prophets will rise and show great signs and wonders to deceive, if possible, even the elect. See, I have told you beforehand."

If we are to beware of 'false prophets', what about false scientists? Celebrity scientists who tell us nothing is knowable, it is all relative, so no one is right or wrong. If that is true, then even the chosen ones (the elect) are being mislead. Although a genius physicist might not know this, why didn't institutional religion condemn atomic research?

Both Einstein and Oppenheimer[2] were nothing but puppets of secular globalists; caricatures of science few people understood. The former, the poster-child of an irreverent form of mass destruction, made physics fun. While the latter was the prototypical mad scientist.

Is it safe to assume physics is an occupation of atheists? Many physicists casually admit to their own lack of faith in a greater being and lead us instead with chaos and anarchy, not in our minds, in theirs.

---

[1] 16th century French oracle who predicted future events.
[2] Scientists associated with the Manhattan Project.

Alchemy

Atheists and their *'God is dead.'*[1] philosophy is best summed up by a physicist who reportedly once said, *"I don't believe in God, I just want to know how the universe was created."*

What can be learned from this attempt to convince Christians that science has answers to creation proving the atheist right? It is a lesson in irony and reverse psychology. The atheist may have their best intentions in mind when they claim to know what does not exist. Allow me to paraphrase a writer who said that in order for an atheist to win an argument, they must know God better than a Christian?

Christians however should know there is a source of doubt in the world and science has won the battle, in a war; a full on assault against a substance that only with faith does it make us free. Their legacy is a contradiction. Doubt and faith don't go together. Doubt weakens faith. And today, the threat of science that created the atomic bomb holds freedom more of a hostage than the vaults at Fort Knox[2].

---

[1] A nihilist belief often attributed to German philosopher Nietzsche.
[2] The US Bullion Depository in Kentucky.

❧ MAGICK OR ALCHEMY OF THE MIND ❦

While I have discussed the use of Alchemy to replace faith with scientific evidence that only a cretinous fool might deny, I thought it would be just as important to include another category requiring faith or, at the very least, a suspension of disbelief in order to succeed.

If magic is a category of harmless entertainment, Magick is a much more serious intrusion into faith. It should not be confused with card game sleights of hand, rabbits pulled from hats or people being sawn in half.

> *"Therefore I speak to them in parables, because seeing they do not see, and hearing they do not hear, nor do they understand."*
>
> Matthew 13:13[2]

Even Christ admits to a creative license in his particular method of instruction. So, I don't exclude the effort of individuals like Paracelsus[1] or the 17th century Rosicrucian movement. I am skeptical when scripture is included; and often more so when it is not. However, I warn against highly influential movements like Freemasons who establish themselves as a hollow form of esoteric ritual with too much leaning toward what is secular.

Since Magick operates on a level of pseudoscience it can trick he participant into believing in something against better judgment because of a lack of better faith. Using

---

[1] (b.1493-1541) Swiss philosopher who influenced the Rosicrucians.

Alchemy

metaphysical or paranormal methods, practiced by mediums, participants are convinced of communication with the dead or that someone is able to relate a future event predicting some favorable or tragic event to an astonished patron. Methods used involved the somewhat dubious practice of telling someone's fortune from dregs after a cup of tea. Palm readers tell the future by studying an open hand. Others promised results from the use of crystal balls or Tarot cards.

Séances, while extremely popular in the 19th century, were the best example of deliberate manipulation in order to get a result. In a darkened room, tables could float. Noises or carefully planned gusts of air against candle flames indicated the presence of a spirit from the 'other side'. Interestingly, a spin-off from Spiritualism and the Occult was the 11th century Chinese Talking or Spirit board, often referred to by its trade name the Ouija board. Originally marketed in the US in 1890 as a toy for children, it was purchased almost exclusively by adults for their own use.

Although considered harmless by most, some of these practices were condemned as paramount to devil worship. And yet, as relates to faith, similar methods were employed to great effect and success by certain individuals.

A few more examples of Alchemy of the Mind include: Joseph Smith, a 19th century American scam artist who fled prosecution in multiple states re-founded Christianity not in the Holy Lands of the Middle East, in upstate New York!

Aleister Crowley, a British occultist and controversial personality in the 1930s invented the cult of Thelema and the use of 'Sex Magick'. L Ron Hubbard, an American science fiction writer never hid the fact he 'invented' a religion in the 1950s still in use today that takes bio-metric readings from a machine to delve deep into the human mind and lessen the harmful effect of 'Thetans'.

the Existential Capitalist

I almost made the mistake of going down the path of an all-too-predictable attack on Communism until I realized Communism and Capitalism can co-exist. The problem with a better economic system is not in any particular form of government, it is Capitalism itself and how it is defined. I don't believe the world in 2025 is Capitalist and no part of Capitalism can exist without a better monetary system. I believe that when we chose paper, we left Capitalism behind because Capitalism is defined by profitability, not an increase in debt. Paper does not deserve to be called money and debt is toxic to profit. Paper may be the promise of payment in money and nothing else.

Let me preface this chapter with the often misunderstood definition of the word 'fascism'? Although the word is often considered 'extremist', it is quite simply secular authority. The word comes from the pre-Roman symbol used to designate a judge or a magistrate. In the not so distant past, it became a militarized movement promoting the rule of law as the highest and final authority. However, despite wars to promote or prevent it, fascism rarely needs either, since in essence it is government and nations only have anarchy

without some semblance of civil order. That is to say, we should not be anti-fascist since that would put us in the chaotic situation of being anti-government.

I'll begin with an icon of the current economic system and a discussion of Russian-American author Ayn Rand's philosophy and her idea of Objectivism. The reason being is I believe the post-war economy in the United States was a combination of different schools of thought I would categorize as Corporate fascism founded on a nationalized banking system obligated to use paper currency. I'll continue with a discussion of literacy, a summary of capital and Capitalism and then a discussion of the Austrian school of thought.

> "I do not surrender my treasures, nor do I share them. The fortune of my spirit is not to be blown into coins of brass and flung to the winds as alms for the poor of the spirit. I guard my treasures; my thought, my will, my freedom. And the greatest of these is freedom."
>
> Equality 7-2521
> *Anthem* (1938)

Although Rand called her philosophy Objectivism, I prefer to place her work in the category of Existential Capitalism. What I mean to say is that she appears to promote laissez-faire, free-will and libertarian ideas, albeit through a secular lens. These ideas are all part of an economic vocabulary. Unfortunately, she lacks any spiritual sense of theory. I find thinly disguised and dissatisfying references to physical desire and almost nothing about the Struggle. So what about morality? She said once that she did not believe morality in individuals can be controlled. If that means legislated, I agree. Until she gives her reason. Her reason is because of the self.

While selfishness is generally considered a bad word, Rand makes it the basis of what many of her readers consider the definition of Capitalism. I agree and I also disagree. If the self is our mortal being, then we are materialistic in seeking to satisfy desire of the self. If however, we are guided by the spirit, I believe we should use caution and instead be aware of judgment for our sin.

I find human arrogance is quite common among agnostics, atheists and militant evangelicals. However, secularism is a serious deception related to Capitalism when it attracts, as Rand does, people who look for a better faith.

I don't mean to belittle her effort, I say Rand should not be ignored. She is not what I would call fascist. There are no heroes for justice or the State. Law and government are not part of Objectivism. She doesn't preach from a pulpit and doesn't invoke any religious doctrine. She is more Orwellian[1], dystopian without an overt social or political commentary.

So what is her appeal? I believe she possessed the ability to project what Jung[2] called an archetype into characters she created, usually male. I discuss my personal view of human

---

[1] George Orwell, writer of *Animal Farm* and *1984*.
[2] Austrian psychoanalyst who disagreed with Freud and his theory of character development.

character within the chapter entitled *The Eternal Spirit* and suggest that Rand may have occupied the category Paternal and therefore, if type A or type II, was she torn between matriarchal and patriarchal guidance?

Mises[1] reportedly said she was, *"The most courageous man in America."* It is true the emphasis in her writing is on men and mankind and rarely makes any substantive comment on anything feminine or female. She appears to be a traitor to feminists yet not acknowledged by the male dominated Pantheon of politics, economics or theology.

This lack of recognition is unfortunate. Because of the projections from her own psyche, I believe Rand should be recognized as an archetype herself. Someone post-war America desperately needed to justify an economy increasingly based on fiat.

---

[1] Economist and member of the Austrian school.

❧ INTELLECTUALS & THE PRINTING PRESS ❧

It might be difficult to convince anyone that a barrier to a better monetary system was in fact one of the greatest benefits to human civilization ever: the printing press. This is especially true since we know that one of the most celebrated works ever published and printed on early presses were Bibles. It was the movable type printing press that made knowledge more accessible than ever before to a broader spectrum of the population. The sense of being in control of one's destiny simply because of access to information that could be processed by more human minds than the literate minority who preceded it was a benefit to humanity, not a hindrance. Knowledge empowered more individuals to make decisions for themselves and together with each other collectively. The path of freedom was formed from the intellectual strength of being better informed. It is undeniable literacy taught skill and talent, and those things led to progress and invention.

However, the literacy and intellectual confidence among the so called 'ignorant masses' – agnostics, came with a price. What I refer to is the politically motivated intelligentsia; a social class of individuals who considered themselves intellectually superior because of what they found in printed study. They pursued solitary ambitions that if they had any collective ambition, was both liberal and socialist. Unfortunately, being quite radical might have got them the attention they were seeking but being anti-establishment meant that by the early 20th century they were nothing more than organized chaos.

The combined strength of the intelligentsia eventually led to a worship of a working class hero. While they felt themselves much more empowered as individuals, and each other, they began to question faith, choosing instead to believe in what was provable. In the western world the center of scorn and blame became the Christian religion; a faith science and technology could not prove or disprove and many considered at best an archaic philosophical superstition; a symptom of passive weakness. Accusations were that mind and social control were the methods religion used to control individuals. To the 19th century proletarian, religion only supported a class based system and Christianity was the worst offender.

In Greece, during the fifth century BC, there was a conflict between Athenians and Spartans called the Peloponnesian War. In my mind this was nothing more than a class based conflict between aristocratic intellectuals in Athens and the working class represented by the Spartans. Historians seem to agree Greece was the birthplace of democracy. However, this seems to imply democracy was an answer to conflict within nations by allowing everyone to be part of government. Unfortunately, even after the translation of ancient Jewish scripture into the Greek Septuagint, and although the Athenians won the war, Greece was severely weakened by internal division.

I know this is absurd but suppose Sparta's main objection to Athenian rule was its currency. It is often said that in politics, image is everything. So, while the Greeks got an owl on their coins, Romans got Caesar. Then they got an answer to a better social order – a hybrid of aristocracy and democracy based on Jewish scripture in Jerusalem. This then gave way to aristocratic European monarchies and eventually democracy or, as Plato[1] said, the 'rule of the poor'. If Plato meant poor in the sense of a lack of faith instead of a lack of money, then we have failed for a very long time to recognize the foundation of a better monetary system.

Fast forward to the 19th century and history appears to repeat itself when, with gold and silver in circulation, religious institutions didn't appear to offer any better application of Christian faith. Instead, a philosophical school of thought would create the idea of a working class hero, the 'Ubermensch' (Ger. Superman) and turn everyone against Christendom. A machine age would attempt to direct nations toward a nihilistic belief in mankind's superiority over the past, allowing us to reshape a new future of our own design.

We were attempting, and succeeding, to usurp the moral understanding of knowing right from wrong from a greater authority; remaking a new authority from a fantasy of fiction. The result was a secular union serving the proletariat but carrying a steep price: denial of the Spirit. Despite the fact that those who denied Christ might have had pre-Christian Messianic heroes in mind, they were junk

---

[1] Ancient Greek writer of *The Republic* c.375 BC.

food for a malnourished youth; a poor substitute for Christ continued today in comic books and popular fiction. Something no amount of cheap entertainment can invent will prevent what Scripture makes clear – denying the Spirit is a sin that never gets forgiven.

The product of the Intelligentsia is actually ignorance, an ignorance of faith. Not preserving things of the past that must be continued going forward. The State replaced faith in the family and the individual. Religion was to blame for any and all wars and conflict. We were taught peace and how we are all saved by the alleged truth of science. However, there have been more wars in the name of peace than in Christ and none claimed to be in defense of a Spirit. Scientific inquiry has branched off in many directions, mixing and merging with industry, manufacturing, medicine, healthcare, art, entertainment and so on; effectively pulling minds away from any continued understanding of faith.

> "It has been considered as of so much importance that a proper number of young people should be educated for certain professions, that, sometimes the public, and sometimes the piety of private founders have established many pensions, scholarships, exhibitions, bursaries, etc. for this purpose, which draw many more people into those trades than could otherwise pretend to follow them. In all christian countries, I believe, the education of the greater part of churchmen is paid for in this manner. Very few of them are educated altogether at their own expense. The long, tedious, and expensive education, therefore, of those who are, will not always procure them a suitable reward, the church being crowded with people who, in order to get employment, are willing to accept of a

> much smaller recompense than what such an education would otherwise have entitled them to; and in this manner the competition of the poor takes away from the reward of the rich."

Although ambivalent about a preference for any specific religious denomination, Adam Smith appears to lament a 'brain drain' from an imbalance in Europe between labor and stock. Whether it was a criticism or a simple statement of fact, Smith felt intelligent minds had been drawn away from the Church in favor of more lucrative positions in secular institutions. His theory that Christianity would be better served if it was better paid seems materialistic. Yet it was in England until Henry VIII, the dissolution of the monasteries and the Reformation, that those voluntary contributions to Catholicism got religion accused of being a threat. The idea of any church, not just Rome having more property and wealth than the English Crown could raise in taxes was a major argument for an end to patronage, even though a lot of Catholic property had been granted by estates and titled heads, some of which were monarchs.

However, despite the fact the intelligentsia appeared to offer a better solution and secular thought has become ingrained in all areas of society, their roots were not in a faith founded on a belief in something. They were in fact basing their faith on a nihilistic belief in nothing.

❧ THE POLITICAL ECONOMY ✥

Anyone who has more than a pedestrian interest in economics must have heard of certain characters who have shaped our understanding of political economy. If a list does not include at least Adam Smith, then it should also recognize the effort of Thomas Malthus, David Ricardo, Jean-Baptiste Say or James Mill.

What is political economy? Political economy is the turning point at which most monetary matters related to finance and banking became less private and more public. The point at which many governments became more interested in the mechanics of the economy. In England in the 18th century, the transition started with the move from an agrarian to an industrial economy and with laws and debates about rent and corn (wheat, barley and rye). Since most private land at the time was in the hands of large estates, discussions about rent offered a solution to the cost of production of an essential human need and how to provide for a growing population. In agrarian politics, the issue was how much burden had been placed on the common people and how much better it would be if they were compensated with profits from land they owned.

There were opinions on both sides of the aisle resulting in what would later be called mercantile. A government policy of protectionism was a defense against too many imports with a balance of trade in favor of a net increase in exports.

Unfortunately, in hindsight it is easy to see that no difference was made from the private ownership of land that a farmer worked for their own profit or loss and laws either protecting the domestic production of corn by allowing or not the importation of cheaper corn from abroad. However, that would not prevent governments from even more intrusion into what had hitherto been private.

Oddly enough, in hindsight it is easy to see that no difference was made from the private ownership of land that a farmer worked for their own profit or loss and laws either protecting or not the domestic production of corn by allowing or not the importation of cheaper corn from abroad. That wouldn't prevent governments from even more intrusion into what had hitherto been private.

Freedom and being in control of one's economic future is a cornerstone of capitalism. The irony in having deeds or titles to property meant individual mortgages only contributed more to accumulated debt. As the economy became industrial, the total amount of sovereign debt was decreased with a larger share going to personal or household debt. The trend was encouraging individuals to be themselves liable for national debt. To put it in other words, debt was being distributed and becoming democratic. Debt was becoming the great equalizer. Although it would take some time, debt would be the means by which individuals and families could appear to be prosperous and upwardly mobile. credit would feel on par with an individual with a title and there would be less need to be taught morality, only law and justice

Scripture may have been the domain of the Church, credit was going to be the key to a proletarian government.

What I find interesting in this part of history from the perspective of my theory is the relationship of Thomas Malthus and David Ricardo.

Thomas Malthus was a Cambridge academic who became a member of the Anglican Church. In 1798, he wrote a well-known and influential book about population and food supply.

David Ricardo was born of Jewish immigrants from Portugal whose father became very well off in England in the snuff and tobacco trade. It was from this business at a very young age I believe Ricardo developed a knack for commodity trading which allowed him to be almost unbelievably successful in banking and investment. Although proof of the type of banking and investment he was so good at is scarce, it appears to have been primarily securities with capital held in trust.

Ricardo appears to be the fictional model of any young lad who, with optimistic determination becomes a success by proving what characteristics are necessary to achieve success. He is the embodiment of free market and laissez-faire capitalism. Despite the admiration even I might have for him, the questionable nature of his success is it came in large part from investments in war debt, of which I am sure must have created an inner conflict and may have been the reason for his later interest in economics and his association with many writers and politicians including his 'camaraderie' with Malthus.

However, I detect or perhaps suspect in his writing that he may have been consciously looking for both a purpose and a reason for his easy success. I don't believe his marriage to a Quaker and his conversion to Unitarianism were accidental. Nor was his long time relationship with a well-educated member of the Anglican Church.

After the Napoleonic Wars in 1815, Ricardo accepts there is no more to be made in dealing with government securities and decides to retire. Despite the fact that he appears to have moved his investments into real estate, he cannot see into the future how profitable debt will be. Seemingly baffled as to how he became Sheriff of Gloucestershire, he later purchases a seat in Parliament after which he tells Malthus he is not sure what issues he should present and even confesses finding public speaking difficult. After trying to take a lead from other members of Parliament, Ricardo takes issue with what he is most familiar with, the Bank of England.

> "I always enjoy any attack on the Bank, and if I had sufficient courage I would be party to it."

Ricardo's attack on the very institution that made him a success reminds me of an angry mob finally gaining entrance to an almost empty Bastille[1] or Luther* founding a church in his name, and then preferring beer, philosophy and married life instead; proving like Babbitt[2] that success might be a failed attempt at being an individual.

Malthus had already written *An Essay on the Principle of Population* (1798) about the food supply and made speeches in Parliament. Since there appeared to be no threat from overpopulation, only how to feed more people, Malthus excludes nature and only offers advice from the human perspective. Whether Malthus' advice is agreeable or critical, Ricardo never seems satisfied. Ricardo's humility is plenty reason to doubt his material success always proves him right. However, much of Ricardo's criticism in one letter is tempered in the next so it may have been simply the dodge and parry of friendly debate.

> "I fear I shall not have the satisfaction of receiving your acquiescence to my doctrines, particularly as I have reverted to my former views respecting taxes on raw produce. Whatever may be correct on that subject, surely Adam Smith is wrong, as there are various passages in his book inconsistent with each other."

Letter 3rd January, 1817

Unfortunately, the gospel according to Adam Smith can go no further in correcting the poverty and slums of the industrialized towns. Discussions about the national debt's deflationary effect offers emigration as just about the only

---

[1] Prison in Paris stormed at the start of the French Revolution in 1789.
* See Index.
[2] Title character of a book published in 1922.

solution. Although the future has proved that more shiny metal won't solve every crisis, Ricardo believes the Bank of England should be less private and purchase more gold.

Ricardo even flip-flops in a letter of 17th October, 1815 with the idea of abolishing the gold standard. He writes on 25th May, 1818, asking if it might be better the Bank of England pay a dividend on its stock rather than purchase more gold since the latter, *"might be attended with the most serious consequences to widows, orphans, and others"*. Unfortunately, any response from Malthus to such a question might appear callous and cynical when posed from someone who made their fortune from war. Perhaps Ricardo meant well and his later service in government was an act of gratitude and of penance?

Without a better answer from any member of institutional religion, we are left with a material fixation and the glorification of certain metals without an understanding of what is essentially a system of faith and nature – both of ourselves and the nature around us. I can't help becoming socialist when I ask myself what we should expect when labor earns and saves and yet finds itself destitute because of the naivete of a select few?

To wit, I present the following quote from a letter to Ricardo written after a recent visit to Ireland:

> *"The face of the country is in many parts very uninteresting from the want of hedges and trees in the inclosures[sic]; but other parts are not deficient in trees, and often present grand and fine features.*

> *Nothing indeed can be more beautiful than Killarney, and Glengariff, a part of Bantry bay. The county of Wicklow also which I saw afterwards by myself is extremely picturesque and beautiful."*

Is it with regret that Malthus becomes less poetic?

> *"The Land in Ireland is infinitely more peopled than in England; and to give full effect to the natural resources of the country, a great part of this population should be swept from the soil into large manufacturing and commercial Towns."*

Is Malthus promoting the idea that nature could be improved with human invention in a land that historically presented a real difficulty to the Anglican Union? I believe this is less of a religious debate than agrarian versus industrial economics. If an Anglican argues in favor, does a Catholic argue against? I'll only add that I find social organization tends to flatter mankind at the expense of nature. So, let us ponder the idea that if a country, like an individual, has a collective identity, did the effort to integrate Ireland into the UK retard Ireland's future development and threaten its cultural heritage?

What is interesting in some of Ricardo's letters is the mention of another well-known economist Jean-Baptiste Say. Say and his family were French Protestants who before the secular revolution were forced to move to Switzerland. Say aligns himself with Adam Smith and although Ricardo mentions him from time to time, I cannot find a reference to Say in Malthus' works. My thoughts are religion played a significant role in economic decision making in England.

Perhaps maintaining the monarchy was maintaining the status quo. Put another way, perhaps Malthus thought it better from the point of view of revolution to not comment on certain aspects of the economy or the monetary system.

Say did however attempt to raise political economics to an exact science even if one of his most well known books was a 'Catechism'. Is his use of this particular word religious? He is almost Biblical in his choice of language in response to common land ownership: *"In the same way that we procure fruit when we do not possess the tree that bears it."* Despite 'Catechism' having an air of indoctrination about it, Say was balanced on a tightrope and a precarious path towards Communism when discussing how much control labor should have over capital; an idea that would be continued by Marx and Engels.

Unfortunately, when Say's theories are not about the economy and rather the monetary system, they have the depth of a teaspoon. That being the case, it is worth mentioning Libertarians and their fixation on heroic idealism lest we forget that finance for the French Revolution was mostly theft, appropriation, forced loans and defaults. The exact reasons why France lost its position as the world's most credible lender and then tried to assert its right to maintain that position by attempting to invade all of Europe!

❧ CAPITAL & CAPITALISM ❦

In order to continue my discussion on existential capitalism, it is necessary to discuss Communism and give my definition of a few terms: Capital and Capitalism.

Capital is the accumulation of large amounts of idle wealth; wealth not borrowed, neither invested nor owed. It is money or property lawfully attributed to a person or institution.

On the other hand, Capitalism is the use of capital for profit. Collective nouns refer to herds and flocks and might also refer to humans. Examples are trusts, cartels and syndicates who attempt to distribute profit to their members as much as labor unions. They only differ in name.

Although Proletarians were taught by Libertarians that a Capitalist is a common enemy, the word has since become almost trendy given that so many young upwardly-mobiles derive income from passive and retail investment. Even though individual and institutional trusts were frowned upon, a public monopoly of the very same banking and financial system was not. Private banking is fine just not when Congress must queue up in line at a teller's window along with everyone else. God forbid they are refused even more credit when they couldn't possibly repay what they already owe. If that should happen, debt becomes somewhat ironic since Libertarians will eventually find it more difficult, if not impossible, to govern given the mountain of liability legislators have already created on their citizen's behalf.

Yet, in the late 19th century, being a Capitalist meant becoming a pariah; the scorn and blame of anything and everything. As legitimate as some of the concerns were, labor, both nationally and internationally, appears to have never been more likely to rebel against the businesses that employed them. However it may have seemed, was the 'establishment', as it was often called, Capitalist and did it only prefer a status quo?

> "The existence of a class which possesses nothing but the ability to work is a necessary presupposition of capital.
>
> It is only the dominion of past, accumulated, materialized labour over immediate living labour that stamps the accumulated labour with the character of capital.
>
> Capital does not consist in the fact that accumulated labour serves living labour as a means for new production. It consists in the fact that living labour serves accumulated labour as the means of preserving and multiplying its exchange value."

Karl Marx*
Wage, Labour and Capital (1849)

According to the prophet of Communism, capital is not accumulated wealth, it is labor itself. Unfortunately, a caveat: labor must work to maintain the value of capital accumulated in the past. History proves a commodity based system of exchange with a fixed denomination will maintain its value over time without inflation. From 1800 to the 1940s, given inflation and deflationary forces, pricing in the US was relatively flat around a baseline. After 1940, the plot

---

* See Index.

line is quite dramatically different. Some sources answer that the dramatic increase and decrease in prices was simply the result of a normal 'business cycle'. Although nature – human or otherwise, can create peaks and troughs, government has almost always had the most dramatic effect. I find that both peaks and troughs accompany times when there was too much currency in circulation. There seems to be an argument of which preceded the other and is therefore to blame. Since this is a complicated topic, I can only state for the sake of my theory that a political decision was made between labor and capital with a government compromise dumping way too much gold and silver into circulation.

Both capital and labor suffered a compromise for materialistic reasons that sacrificed a better faith. Unfortunately, unbeknownst to them, this presented a serious problem. In order for anything to be capital and this includes labor, it must be, or must be able to be, converted into wealth. Wealth that is easily exchangeable. That means currency. If labor is also capital, then I have some bad news for mid-century abolitionists; the slavery they opposed was replaced with another. This is because if labor is capital then, like capital, people must be exchangeable; bought and sold.

I believe capitalist, not Marxist economic policies benefit labor. Yet the inverse is part of a political agenda that has persisted for a very long time. Don't believe me? Then I offer a war for freedom financed with paper.

> "Labor is prior to and independent of capital. Capital is only the fruit of labor, and could never have existed if labor had not first existed. Labor is the superior of capital, and deserves much the higher consideration."
>
> Abraham Lincoln
> Message to Congress, 1861

Someone should have told the citizens of Lincoln's day that equality didn't mean freedom. All slaves can be described as equal. All people said to be free are not when they give themselves over to human authority. Where in the Old Testament is morality? Where is the Spirit? I am left wandering in the Old Testament for an answer to the Struggle only found in the New Testament. We should ask ourselves, can we live without Christian guidance? How many nations have the same or similar social order without scripture? Yet, how many people have no guidance from God without Christ? We should all agree law without morality is tyranny and faith without the eternal Spirit is a sin.

ಌ THE ROAD TO SERFDOM ಌ

The title of this section is from a very well known book by the Austrian economist Friedrich Hayek. I find many historians seem to think Keynes was the source of the fiat monetary system but Keynes wanted an international monetary authority located in Switzerland, presumably because the Swiss would never exploit credit to their advantage? I would argue Austrians had greater influence if only because Hayek's polemic against the threat of tyranny from one government is, believe it or not, another government! No one would call Hayek or FDR a fascist unless you dared to accuse them of being Zionist. Even if no one could say exactly how FDR arrived at his conclusions, he may have given Hayek all the material he needed for his book.

Although the economic decisions of the US in the 1930s and 40s were with a group of individuals known as the 'Brain Trust', most were lawyers and none were economists. Critics of that time say FDR overstepped the boundaries of the executive office and the 'brains of the trust' were employed only to find a legal way to circumvent the Constitution and bypass Congress. I am a bit more sympathetic to FDR and his attempt to save democracy. I say the global climate made expedient a national mandate and the climate I refer to was an economy wrecked by debt.

While we are on the subject, why don't we discuss how America fought tyranny with the creation of a dictator. I thought democracy resists authoritarian regimes. I know some people say that democracies don't start wars. And we know that's true because FDR was quoted as once having said that he "hates war". That must be why his reputation has lasted so long, not tarnished in any way by revisionist historians. We shouldn't forget his critics were far more vocal until silenced by the Second World War.

Like war and politics, it's all about image and a good defense. When I learn more about Capitalism from a Marxist than any other source, I am defended from becoming a Communist as long as I don't fall into the trap of believing labor is capital. On the other hand, if I study the Austrians, even if they preach against tyranny, dictatorships and so on, I am well protected in knowing that the monetary system needs an institutional authority separate from government. If I am not protected from both with what I believe then I risk placing myself on either side in a conflict that never ends. No matter how much government may want compromise, compromise only serves the government. We should avoid compromising our belief in freedom because we know what happens when polarity is brought together. Try attaching the positive and negative terminals on a high voltage battery and see what happens. Moving away from a centrist view isn't the answer either. The most extreme in either party will always lead to eventually believing in a consensus when they go from one side of the aisle to the other, swap allegiances and take each other's place.

In order to get a better understanding of the genetic structure of the New World Order, a speech given by FDR in 1941 is worth reprinting in full:

> "In the future days, which we seek to make secure, we look forward to a world founded upon four essential human freedoms.
>
> The first is freedom of speech and expression everywhere in the world.
>
> The second is freedom of every person to worship God in his own way everywhere in the world.
>
> The third is freedom from want which, translated into world terms, means economic understandings which will secure to every nation a healthy peacetime life for its inhabitants everywhere in the world.
>
> The fourth is freedom from fear which, translated into world terms, means a world-wide reduction of armaments to such a point and in such a thorough fashion that no nation will be in a position to commit an act of physical aggression against any neighbor anywhere in the world.
>
> That is no vision of a distant millennium. It is a definite basis for a kind of world attainable in our own time and generation. That kind of world is the very antithesis of the so-called new order of tyranny which the dictators seek to create with the crash of a bomb.
>
> To that new order we oppose the greater conception: the moral order. A good society is able to face schemes of world domination and foreign revolutions alike without fear.
>
> Since the beginning of our American history, we have been engaged in change in a perpetual peaceful revolution; a revolution which goes on steadily, quietly adjusting itself to changing conditions

> without the concentration camp or the quick-lime in the ditch. The world order which we seek is the cooperation of free countries, working together in a friendly, civilized society.
>
> This nation has placed its destiny in the hands and heads and hearts of its millions of free men and women; and its faith in freedom under the guidance of God. Freedom means the supremacy of human rights everywhere. Our support goes to those who struggle to gain those rights or keep them. Our strength is our unity of purpose. To that high concept there can be no end save victory."

FDR was quite clever in the sense he was not telling the whole truth and nothing but the truth. Freedom meant globalists needed a nationalized monetary system. The intended result was disingenuous. In order to fight a future of 'commies everywhere', they were choosing to be fascist.

I use the word fascist not in a critical sense, I use it only as a label for what gives government authority. Any legal authority that is the highest authority could be said to be fascist. Even given the example of Communism, the Politburo or People's Congress is a final legal authority in a single party State and therefore is – fascist.

That does not mean anyone who takes to the street and in protest yells, "DOWN WITH FASCISM!" is stating a preference for clerical government. I am not sure they understand that without social order we have anarchy.

Private banking interests working with legislators put an end to Capitalism when they nationalized the banking industry and then monopolized the monetary system. Until then, citizens had the right to choose a better faith. The right to exercise faith is to choose either our mortal or our immortal being. I laugh at any government promising to make us less afraid. Of whom are we more afraid – bankers? – labor unions? – or secular fascists who work for Zionist one-world government?

However, the reason the US sided with fascism is why I have sympathy for government because if I have already complained labor is not well served when a Marxist suggests that capital is labor and not money, then I have not made any comment on the party at the other end of the spectrum and a country basing its economy on credit. If the US government and the Federal Reserve do not realize they serve a system of publicly traded values then they don't realize how much more gets stolen from labor every day in the stock market and how it is a far greater re-distribution than any welfare program from the New Deal. We should ask ourselves which is more deserving of debt and deficit: labor and low income households or institutions because of their market capitalization? Before you answer, know that in current conditions, the former is far less of a benefit to the government's economy even if both are only possible with a continued faith in a printing press.

It is a sad fact the President talks about a struggle and then fails to mention Christ's name. There is no *"freedom under the guidance of God"* without Christ. We should know the answer to resolving any conflict is faith. I can say with confidence that Christian faith is not part of the Law. Christ did not preach in favor of Law or against it, he brought moral order, faith in the Spirit and what is eternal. I believe it is both compensation for labor and a solution to the Struggle and of knowing right from wrong. Faith is the only freedom there is; faith in the Spirit and Christ's resurrection. If we therefore believe any political party is currently the party of the Pharisees, we should be careful the opposition are not misguided zealots selling the same poison.

Where does this lack of faith lead us? Quite possibly the same place as the Roman empire. After Paul met with Nero and Jerusalem's destruction, Rome began its decline and not because of foreign invasion or civil war. After realizing no more gain from an ever expanding domain, it chose to devalue its currency.

Rome's downfall was its success in becoming an over-extended empire. If the Senate had not pilfered all it had from citizens with inflation, Rome might have been better remembered. Rather than being the pre-eminent example of the folly of humans believing only in themselves or each other, it may have been the template of a future world united. Instead, years of inflation had cheated the entire empire and the peasants were not happy. The lesson is governments should be wary of public sentiment.

Unfortunately, if inflation doesn't get us on the way up, deflation will on the way down. Labor could not make up for what Rome spent, so citizens reacted and became the worse threat to any government there is: apathetic. Rome started as a loosely associated republic and then after becoming an empire, eventually found itself slowly breaking apart. If Judea was a kingdom whose faith was its people, then Plato was almost right, democracy is not far removed from tyranny anywhere in the world.

So little has been written about the economy in those countries when Rome failed and its borders were re-defined. That said, the past has proved the present. The Dark Ages had to have been a very long and deep depression for many people, only offset by the desperate hope of more dependency on legislated authority in the future.

Monetary History

the Golden Dream

Should I argue against gold while trying to convince anyone of my theory? Especially when asking someone to accept that a material object is in fact the substance of a spiritual presence. I might feel the need to argue against a fixation in favor of a fetish. Fetish is after all an emotional need represented with a material object. A fixation is different. A material object takes the place of an emotional need, often times permanently. Neither of these should sound particularly healthy in a rational mind, unless we consider the uncertainty in a fetish stemming from doubt. The real problem is believing the idea that a fixation is an answer and is the truth.

Despite negative connotations and criticism, icons and fetish have existed in religious ceremony for centuries. An example of an icon is a statue or a painting of a Biblical figure. I say the monetary system is a type of fetish when I state that gold is proof of an eternal Spirit. In truth, the Spirit has no physical form, it exists only in what we believe through senses we can not measure or quantify yet our belief in an element's structure creates faith.

From a psychological perspective, a fixation can be the result of a neurosis. An individual may be fixated because of trauma, environmental conditioning or abuse. These problems can lead to a substitution of faith with addiction and self-destructive behavior. The individual can suffer self-esteem and confidence issues, often leading to an individual's need to replace what they choose to believe with rebelliousness or spite. If however, during a crisis of faith, an institution like an individual cannot agree through consensus or conformity, it may display similar symptoms.

Generally speaking a government needs control. I don't argue against a role in creating social order. However, I believe any government seeking more power than necessary by overstepping the limits of its domain into another is not justified in doing so when trying to convince itself of its own sense of self-importance or its own survival when for reasons of free-will, faith might better serve an individual. Governments have come and gone, a better faith to guide us has always been a constant.

This incursion beyond the boundary of what I believe should be delineated is exactly what occurred in banking and the monetary system. However, despite the best effort of government to subvert the currency of any other authority with paper, plastic and potentially even digital, history says highly developed economic systems have never succeeded because of legal mandate or human design. Private systems have generally created better social order when they were accepted by both governments and individuals.

My theory offers faith in the form of Christian wisdom and in practical terms this concept of authority has never with rare exception ever been established. My idea of faith is the idea that metals represent a better Spirit than paper.

I don't mean to condescend silver or be a gold snob, I just find it odd that central banks hold hostage so much gold when silver has over 400+ years of history. The US Treasury has none. The Federal Reserve has none. We have stockpiled a long list of minerals and metals. Everything necessary for national defense, including millions of barrels of oil. Even though not so long ago, the US issued an unbelievable amount in coin and notes, did we completely forget about silver?

Why does this matter? History matters. If we need at some unknown time to secure the monetary system, history says it would most likely not be paper. It might be gold or a combination of metals. Let's not forget that whatever substance we choose, accumulated debt still needs to be paid. Also, if we keep metal in mind, we should remember the US is currently on a copper, nickel, zinc standard. This is something few gold or silver bugs even bother mentioning.

❧ WEIGHTS & MEASURES ☙

It is worth mentioning more than once that a metal system requires a fixed denomination and value. Such a system I believe would also only be stable with a fixed quantity in circulation. I have included chart 12.1 to show a historical association of metal and paper, their foundation and structure. Studying each column carefully, it is possible to note that gold and silver can co-exist with each other when their foundation represents an abstract other than their physical substance. The question is can they co-exist with anything other than metal?

12.1

	The Monetary System		
	A	B	C
Authority	Treasury	Banks	Government
Serves	Aristocratic	Middle-class	Bureaucratic
Currency	Gold	Silver	Paper
Foundation	The Spirit	Labor	Poverty
Result	Capital	Profit	Taxation

The answer is maybe. Fiat can co-exist with commodity based systems until interest rates mean metal has to be devalued or inflation means any more currency only increases debt owed from fiat. This usually results in deflation with a demand for metal and a sell-off of paper.

❧ TIMELINE OF THAT 'OTHER' METAL ☙

I don't think it is necessary to include a complete and comprehensive history of rare earth metals, only a summary. Because the current monetary system is centered in the United States, I am only focusing on silver's heritage in Europe and its legacy in North America.

600 BC: Ancient Greece
The exploitation of mines at nearby Laurion enabled Athens to finance an army and navy, and win control of the Aegean from the Persians. The famous Athenian "Owl" tetradrachm used as currency throughout the Mediterranean was minted from silver mined at Laurion.

200 BC: Hispania
Silver from the Iberian peninsula financed the expansion of the Roman Empire, supplying up to 200 tonnes of silver a year at peak production. These were the largest silver mines in the world until the Spanish conquest of Central and South America.

1545: The New World
Spanish conquistadors discover massive silver deposits in Potosí, Bolivia. The next year, large silver deposits were uncovered in Mexico. Several other silver-bearing areas were also discovered in Peru.

Spanish colonial territory accounted for approximately 85% of global silver production until the early 1800s.

1816: An Empire in Decline

Insolvent after the Napoleonic Wars, the Coinage Act in the UK overvalued gold in a ratio to undervalued silver putting pressure on foreign countries to replace silver.

1859: The Comstock Lode

A large silver discovery in Nevada resulted in an economic boom greater than the California Gold Rush ten years prior. Despite the wealth of silver, nearly half the profits between 1860 and 1880 were from gold.

1863-66: Gresham's Law Becomes Federal Law

'Bad money replaces good', with National Banking Acts placing a 10% tax on private bank notes and Federally chartered credit unions permitted to issue fractional reserve notes at a ratio as low as 5%.

France suffered a humiliating defeat at the hands of Prussia and its allies in the 1870 Franco-Prussian War. As an indemnity, Germany occupied part of France until it paid five billion francs in gold. With a domestic gold standard, German states unified into an empire. Unfortunately, optimism in the German financial sector inflated the economy quite dramatically. After Germany sold off a lot of its silver stock on the open market between 1873 and 1879, deflation led to a decade long depression.

1873: Nations Demonetize

The United States passes the Coinage Act of 1873, halting production of silver dollars.

1875: Paper Rears its Ugly Head

The Specie Payment Resumption Act attempted to convert fiat notes issued during the Civil War into gold. Even though the war ended in 1865, it was discovered in 1875 the Treasury had since then printed even more.

It is not clear what happened to the $450 million in accumulated Northern debt. Although the notes were never recalled, one historian claims, with $300 million still in circulation, when they reached parity with gold, people just 'lost interest' in cashing them in. There seems to be no record of what happened to an estimated $687 million in Southern debt.

The Act also abolished the limit on National Bank notes creating an era of deregulated 'free banking'; giving a competitive edge to a government sponsored franchise.

1878: Dealing With a Threat

Deflation during the 1870s hit American workers and farmers especially hard.

With the US no longer making silver dollars, the 'silver barons' of the Western US lost a loophole that gave them above-average prices for their silver. With the Bland-Allison Act, lobbyists convinced Congress to buy and mint two to four million dollars worth of silver every month. Unfortunately, this subsidy to miners expanded the money supply and made deflation even worse.

Global silver production from 1800 to 1875 quadrupled between 1875 and 1900. This lowered the price of bullion, making the Bland-Allison Act less effective.

1890: The Great Debasement
As silver prices continued to fall, pro-inflation forces aligned and demanded yet again that the government increase its purchases. The result was the Sherman Silver Purchase Act and the Treasury buying 4.5 million ounces a month. This made the US government the world's second-largest buyer of silver after Great Britain.

1893: Financial Panic
An economic depression lasted until 1897, caused by fears that continued silver purchases by the US government would mean paying its debts in silver instead of gold. This led to a dramatic sell-off in stocks and other over-inflated assets for gold coin.

US gold reserves shrunk causing bank failures and high unemployment. President Grover Cleveland managed to repeal the Sherman Silver Purchase Act; reigning in deflation from an already bloated money supply.

1914: The End of Royal Assent
In order to make war more affordable, Britain suspends its gold standard.

A similar standard continued in the United States until 1934.

1918: The Pittman Act

Great Britain was facing a currency crisis. In order to pay considerable war debt, the British government had issued more silver certificates than it had in bullion. The Pittman Act melted 270 of an authorized 350 million dollars sitting unused in US Treasury vaults.

In order to get the backing of Western states in Congress, the Act stipulated that every melted dollar had to be replaced. This began in 1921 and continued until 1935 with a tribute to the Armistice and the Peace Dollar.

1934: Eminent Domain

The Silver Purchase Act of 1934 forced the sale of privately held silver to the government. Aside from circulating coinage, citizens were only allowed to own a certain non-monetary amount.

The US Treasury purchased silver at 50¢/oz – nearly double the market price and issued small denomination notes (certificates) against their stock of $1, $5 and $10; once again increasing the money supply in response to deflation.

1946: US Becomes Top Buyer

The Silver Purchase Act of 1946 ordered the US Treasury to buy silver at the rate of 90.5¢/oz when silver was selling at 87¢/oz. In response, domestic mining tripled.

1959: Global Shortage

The global economy continued its post-WWII boom into the 1950s. Economies destroyed in the war had recovered. Global silver demand increased and in 1959 outpaced production. The US Treasury began selling silver in order to keep prices under $1.29/oz.

By the mid-1960s, the US would become the world's leading source of silver.

1961: Over the Limit

When global silver prices rose above 91¢/oz in 1961, orders flowed in at below-market prices. President Kennedy ordered a halt to government silver sales and the retirement of $5 and $10 certificates.

With the US no longer capping silver prices, they continued their ascent.

1964: Melt Value Increases

Hoarding became an issue as silver prices went above $1.29/oz in 1963.

Between 1933 and 1962, demand had gone from 10 to 110 million ounces annually causing prices to rise. Coin hoarding meant there was a desperate shortage of dimes, quarters, and half dollars. As soon as the US Mint released new coins, they disappeared.

The Treasury eventually exhausted its supply of silver dollars and honored redemptions with bags of silver granules.

1965: Removed from Coinage
Congress passes the Coinage Act of 1965; adjusting and removing silver in circulation.

1968: Certificates Retired
The government decides to recall the last of the Treasury silver certificates – the one dollar. As they came in, they were destroyed and replaced with Federal Reserve notes. While they still continue to be legal tender, they can no longer be redeemed in silver.

1970: Demonetized
This was the last year of the half dollar with 40% silver and the last year of any coin with a silver content intended for circulation.

I recognize there is a slightly irrational bias in favor of gold. I believe we should teach its role along side other metals in a Christian monetary system. But, after considerable research, I am willing to concede that the award for global economic stability isn't, despite the short lived Bretton Woods agreement, the ever elusive and permanent gold standard. Let's not forget, rarity of a metal does not always imply a stable system and silver was a standard for much longer. Today, central banks continue to collectively obsess over the shiny metal yet coins in the US are mostly alloys of other elements – copper, nickel and zinc.

China

China has not always been communist. Before one of Europe's most influential intellectual exports made its way to Asia, China had perhaps the first highly developed monetary system, which didn't exist until China had an emperor, a skilled productive workforce and profitable foreign trade. Merchants, not government, needed spending authority and a stable medium of exchange. Government in turn needed social order. So a compromise appears to have occurred between the systems of credit and exchange.

Legend has it China was the first country in the world to use fiat currency and it was an absolute disaster. However, legend may be wrong since paper was in use in China for such a long period of time. We know for a fact however that fiat has since gained the undeniable reputation of creating inflation and uncertainty in economic systems. Yet there appears to be no evidence of tension between public and private interests as one might expect or as much inflation as economic instability might imply if there had been an exclusively fiat system.

Most research concludes that inflation was the result of the government particularly during the Yuan[1] dynasty printing too much currency without value attached to it. This caused inflation. Yet historical accounts from the 13th century only acknowledge a devaluation in the currency from government sources. Citizens, merchants and visitors from outside China say the currency was extremely stable and according to Marco Polo[2] was *"as good as gold"*.

Money is often defined as a means of exchange and provided it doesn't physically deteriorate over time, it is a reliable store of value. Paper currency can be a means of exchange although because of the tendency to overprint and inflation, is never the latter for very long. However, I believe if citizens are able to convert fiat into a non-volatile commodity, then an economy has a means of exchange (even if paper) and a store of value. Of course, the commodity has to be recognized as superior in some way in order to justify the cost of exchange.

There is a lack of understanding the effect of too much currency in circulation and what a fiat system is. A commodity can be the cause of inflation if it doesn't compensate labor when it enters into circulation. Fiat, on the other hand, is the very definition of inflation itself. This is why some historians attribute inflation in China with too much of a good thing. The arrival of silver from large finds in Peru and the Philippines could have increased the money supply at a pace exceeding the ability of labor and business

---

[1] Emperors from 1271 to 1368. Also a unit of Chinese currency.
[2] Italian whose book *The Travels of Marco Polo* c.1300 described China during the Yuan dynasty.

to produce enough goods and services without raising prices. Yet precious metals are rarely accused of causing inflation unlike paper currencies. Too many historians present conflicting views. They side with either public debt or private wealth being at fault or one and not the other being the solution. Rarely, if ever, do they consider both systems might work together. I used to think the answer to economic instability was hard currency, or gold. I had an intolerance for theories supporting paper. Although, after considering the early Chinese economy, I have to say I don't have more respect for fiat, I have a better understanding of public and private co-operation.

Fiat, the currency conjured out of nothing is synonymous with inflation. Inflation is both profit and interest used to repay the loan. The gain on the investment will continue to diminish even after it is repaid because inflation always demands an exponential increase. It is a system which should be avoided not only because it takes from labor, it requires taking from labor. If the money supply is increased, inflation reduces the value of compensation labor receives. If the issuer thinks themselves more responsible, interest is applied in order to repay and effectively remove the currency from circulation. Unfortunately, deflation also affects the occupations of labor.

I wanted to show the basic premise that if debt equals inflation they both result in downward pressure on wages and employment. While I am not a classically trained economist, I thought I would see if such an equation already existed. I have included a few I found that might better illustrate a contradiction that exists in political economy of paper versus metal and fiat versus a commodity based system of exchange.

The Phillips Curve

$$\pi_t = \beta \, \epsilon_t [\pi_t + 1] + \kappa [m_t - p_t]$$

The New Keynesian Curve

$$\pi_t = \beta \, \epsilon_t [\pi_t + 1] + \kappa [m_t - p_t]$$

These types of equations pop up from time to time in economic research and are the bread and butter of academic discussion. It might be difficult for the untrained eye to notice a difference since the difference is so subtle I am told, and only becomes obvious when 'interpreted'.

However, in order to save time, one of the curves shows a positive correlation between credit, growth and employment. The other curve shows the negative impact of debt, inflation and unemployment. One was developed to explain the post-war British economy. The other was further developed to explain stagflation in the 1970s. Only one is desirable in an economy, the other every economist would recommend avoiding. Although they only appear to differ in name, mathematicians often create worlds where logic and reason seem to no longer exist.

We should remember that if too much currency of any commodity, paper or metal, enters circulation without value attached to it, then inflation and a downward pressure on employment are the result – hence the equation. This can occur even when using metals. Yet in China this did not appear to be the case. Why, what was their secret? And why keep using paper if it constantly caused such problems? China used these systems from the 9th until the mid-15th century. Five hundred or so years. If fiat is a mistake, why did we not learn from the error of human judgment? They must have had a method of taming its ill effect.

Because my research is limited, I would guess if the Chinese government monopolized the precious metals market, it could control the volume of silver and the rate at which it was converted to paper because the public sensing the effect of inflation, could refuse government paper. Neither however could resist a demand for foreign goods and finding themselves short of silver. If too much currency causes inflation, then too little might explain a recession. Although both inflation and a recession are undesirable economic conditions, if they oscillate around a base line does one or other of those formulas explain a healthy economy?

So why did China stop using fiat exchange? There is no clear answer. Although not perfect it was an almost intuitive balance between government and the people. Attempts to revive the fiat system in the 19th century proved quite catastrophic in China. Similar systems in India and Persia also failed. My theory is that by the time of the Ming[1]

---

[1] Emperors from 1368 to 1644.

dynasty, China's economic system was exclusively based on hard currency, or to be more precise, silver. We often believe a rare earth element should provide more stability, yet by the early 1500s while silver was becoming an international standard, it was also beginning to show its weaknesses. Was that because government began relying more on taxation in order to control spending? The Yuan system was a yin-yang between the domains of public and private economy; the former threatened by less revenue from taxation and the latter, unemployment. The system would fail unless both tolerated each other. However, the Ming dynasty's exclusive use of silver was the beginning of China's slow decline. Did they make the mistake of restricting credit too much leaving the country without enough room to expand?

I believe economies in the past have failed when there weren't co-operative systems of exchange between public and private. There are dangers in being entirely intolerant of each other. Good examples are arguments against silver by gold bugs or government condemnation of excessive wealth and banks refusal to lend to public institutions.

Unfortunately, if making a money supply 'elastic' can only be accomplished with debt, the lesson from history in the Yuan era is that citizens should have had faith in a private monetary system. I believe if democracy is freedom of choice, then citizens should have been taught what the risks are of debt and governments should have defended the right to make that choice.

Parliament & Democracy

The United States, or America, is not actually American. America is the product of a free thought movement in Europe which preceded its establishment in the centuries after the invention of the printing press. Probably the best example of this broad appeal of liberalism prior to the Revolution in 1776 is a pamphlet called *Common Sense*. Although simplistic and naive, it did represent the evolution of serf and peasant to commoner and then later to what I call 'proletarian'.

After the Revolution, the process was continued with a book called *The Rights of Man*. Written by Thomas Paine who single-handedly embodied much of the spirit of the American experiment. We shouldn't forget the efforts of Francis Bacon, John Locke and Issac Newton; all of whom, third president of the United States, Thomas Jefferson said were: *"the three greatest men that have ever lived"*. Why does that matter? Because it was high praise from someone of such stature.

However, for the sake of my theory, I have to say none of those named are from scripture. And why would they? The founding members of government were promoting social rules that implied a political construct. It was secular European idealism and an intellectual elite ignoring class based differences; shaping the desire of both the proletariat and the wealthy, making vague promises of subjective concepts of life and liberty.

I have to add that by the 17th century there was good reason for abandoning monarchy. The best example is probably the most tragic. Since at least the time of the pharaohs in ancient Egypt, there has been a tendency for human authority to think itself on an equal level with God(s). When they have, arrogance and conceit might make them appear indistinguishable. The sad part is that he was the son of James VI, working on the advice of his father made to his brother about the role of divine right. James wrote a book called *Basilika Doron* (*Royal Gift*) which laid out the principles of being a king that was best summarized in a speech given in 1610:

> "The state of monarchy is the supremest thing upon earth, for kings are not only God's lieutenants upon earth and sit upon God's throne, but even by God himself, they are called gods."

I wouldn't pity Charles I for his indiscretion if he wasn't also the son of the man who authorized the most well-known edition of the Bible in the English language.

The problem I have with this is that I believe the symbolic authority of the crown is the spiritual resting on the temporal and a monarch's relationship with the Church.

Be that as it may, by the late 18th century, success in colonial America would become a determination to cut ties with Great Britain and be independent of Europe. Intellectual justification was a good start. Unfortunately, in order to be truly free, few professors of history will tell students a new monetary system had to be included. Also, in justifying order from chaos, a new identity would have to replace the heritage of the people that would populate the land. So while historians often discuss the 'melting pot', they rarely if ever include the necessity of faith in anything other than the rule of law. This results in a problem: how did pre-revolutionary idealists convince colonists they needed a violent overthrow of power yet not discuss securing financing? History tells us little more was said about the reason for a conflict other than 'taxation without representation'. Taxation is certainly a political motive, yet should we exclude faith?

Consider what Adam Smith said in 1776, the first year of the new republic:

> "The Americans, it has been said, indeed, have no gold or silver money, the interior commerce of the country being carried on by a paper currency; and the gold and silver, which occasionally come among them, being all sent to Great Britain, in return for the commodities which they receive from us. But without gold and silver, it is added, there is no possibility of paying taxes. We already get all the gold and silver which they have. How is it possible to draw from them what they have not?
>
> The present scarcity of gold and silver money in America, is not the effect of the poverty of that country, or of the inability of the

people there to purchase those metals. In a country where the wages of labour are so much higher, and the price of provisions so much lower than in England, the greater part of the people must surely have wherewithal to purchase a greater quantity, if it were either necessary or convenient for them to do so. The scarcity of those metals, therefore, must be the effect of choice, and not of necessity.

It is for transacting either domestic or foreign business, that gold or silver money is either necessary or convenient."

...

"The redundancy of paper money necessarily banishes gold and silver from the domestic transactions of the colonies ..."

...

"In the exterior commerce which the different colonies carry on with Great Britain, gold and silver are more or less employed, exactly in proportion as they are more or less necessary. Where those metals are not necessary, they seldom appear. Where they are necessary, they are generally found."

Was the revolution really about freedom? If so, then how was that freedom defined? It would appear the freedom not being discussed is in reality gold and silver. And the American colonies appear not to have enough of it to transact foreign exchange, including paying taxes. As for the representation the colonies claim they do not have, Smith mentions that in Britain there was as much concern representatives from the colonies would have a greater influence on domestic British policy. So much concern in fact, that some British wanted to let them go without a fight.

We shouldn't forget that the basic tenets of the 'rights of man' intellectual movement was the product of a greater period of European enlightenment. Even the most stubborn or ignorant are even more stubborn and ignorant if they don't at least nod their head to the idea that all humans are created equal. And what would make them even more equal than anyone else, Christian faith or a better monetary system? No, the future in mind was democracy and jurisprudence.

The argument I have against common rule is I believe a country guided by faith brings heritage and history. Democracy, on the other hand, is a vote among the common people for what can be taken away.

Those huddled masses arriving were in large part economic migrants, refugees from poverty who would populate a land and live under a secular government boldly advertising itself as a separation of Church and State. Because if anything gets in the way of a pilgrim's progress, it has to be religion. Sarcasm aside, ask anyone if Church and State are separate, and they may be in agreement until you remind them the word secular actually means atheist. Then they might pause for thought.

As for paying for war; why question independence? Doesn't noble effort finance itself? If so, the profit of freedom would repay its obligation many times over. The United States would become a micro-cosmic dream; an embryonic incubator of freedom; a model for every other nation. Everyone would willingly accept debt on behalf of Liberty, unless they did not want any part of the revolution. So, the Continental, a debt based currency, only worth the paper it was printed on, was issued to pay for militias, uniforms, weapons and all the rest. A war by a nation with no way to pay for it.

However, there did exist a proverbial 'deal with the devil'. Although lacking faith in anything of value, fiat currency could be borrowed from the future, conjured from thin air. So, given the increase in currency without a corresponding increase in value within the economy, by the end of the war, inflation followed hot on its heals.

Sure, the Continental had been counterfeited by the British as part of their war effort. But inflation, it should be noted, whether you have enemies or not, occurs as a form of theft from labor, by the people or institutions who issue the debt. Who cares if you lie and tell people it's money? What is the true price of freedom?

Starting off on the right foot, Article I of the Constitution of the United States as it was written in 1789 appeared to lay the foundation of a better monetary system:

> *"No State shall enter into any Treaty, Alliance, or Confederation; grant Letters of Marque and Reprisal; coin Money; emit Bills of Credit; make any Thing but gold and silver Coin a Tender in*

> Payment of Debts; pass any Bill of Attainder, ex post facto Law, or Law impairing the Obligation of Contracts, or grant any Title of Nobility."

Was the Federal government being given control of the monetary system or was that an imposition of a rule related to a right within each State? Rather than choosing faith in something other than government, some semblance of a stable monetary system was included in the rules, if only with exception, leaving the final decision on whether to honor that to Congress, which they did not in 1913 with the Federal Reserve Act. Since Federal Reserve notes are Treasury notes printed under contract, the central bank of the United States has authority over every other treasury in the Federal domain. That means States lost to a currency based on credit. How long, after fifty years of fiat, until the Federal Reserve itself loses control?

Is this like something from Revelation? A creature borne aloft on bat-like wings with the promise of humanitarian public service; in flight, laying waste with fire and flame letting her brood pick the bones of dead industry while vulture capitalists[1] patiently wait their turn to clean up with mergers and acquisitions.

Leaving aside that apocalyptic vision, it would appear there still exists no amendment to justify replacing the explicit requirement in Article I of a bi-metallic standard. So when FDR and then Nixon ignored Article I, executive orders could override Congress while turning a blind eye on the

---

[1] The scrap merchants of insolvency.

Constitution since respecting Article I might have exposed an insolvent federal government. Democracy might have been saved but where is freedom today?

> *"Think not that I am come to send peace on earth: I came not to send peace, but a sword. For I am come to set a man at variance against his father, and the daughter against her mother, and the daughter in law against her mother in law."*
>
> Matthew 10:34-35[1]

And that leads to the subject of why a Civil War in 1861 was inevitable – because of the king. The king being cotton. In the 1850s a worldwide glut had developed in the organic fiber and being the backbone of the southern agricultural economy, less demand meant stockpiles were left to rot. This crisis presented such an enormous risk of default in the North that independence of the US may have been put at risk if such a default meant capital markets in Europe had to suffer. So, four score and some odd years after the Revolution, the issue was not preservation of the Union, it was how a country could finance a war with itself before another nation got involved. Lucky for us, European nations were all engaged in conflicts in other parts of the world and their textile industries had other sources of raw material in Egypt and India.

If people were convinced of the necessity of war, why was it so difficult to finance? That was because no private capital in the North felt compelled by any argument that they would willingly invest in a conflict affecting commerce and free trade between them. Although Cooke's[1] somewhat novel idea of going 'door-to-door' and direct selling very small blocks of Treasury securities was something of an innovation.

However, since technological innovation was making slavery less attractive to investors, a war with the South might have meant even less margin of profit and a guarantee of a very large default of money already owed to the Second bank of the United States which might have soured relations with foreign capital abroad. There would also be the moral and ethical considerations of an honorable conflict.

If paper could not be used to pay taxes, could a Treasury note be used as currency? Since the independence of a still youthful nation was at stake, the Greenback was introduced. Although popular among citizens, the notes came with a bold 'promise to pay' on them yet no indication what anyone would receive in exchange.

Interestingly, in the first year of the war, over a third of government revenue in the Confederate South came from donations. Even though the public appeared eager for war, I don't believe either side wanted to accept the root cause of the conflict was financial. After a prohibition on the importation of slaves in 1807, slavery had become such an unprofitable institution, I believe the real cause was unmanageable levels of unpaid (paper) debt. Some sources claim that the Confederate Congress in a last-ditch attempt allegedly 'threatened' a gold standard. They told banks they

---

[1] American broker who helped finance the Union during the US Civil War.

should stop converting government currency into bank notes. How much truth there is in this I do not know. However, I believe that threat would only make sense if bank vaults were filled with something more of value than paper. People tend to hoard cash in uncertain times so maybe the banks held more bullion than the government. If so, the Confederacy was losing the war and the faith of the people. Which came first is not entirely clear.

You might be asking yourself why the need for a fiat currency? Good question. The reason was that until the First World War, money markets were a very exclusive club and governments couldn't sell the idea of war to anyone unless they bought their bonds. Despite the risk of not being paid from either side at war's end, both the North and South did finance a lot of debt abroad. Also, unlike the Greenback, some issues of Southern currency offered interest. However, they relied on foreign investor confidence lost in the wake of destruction when Sherman[1] marched through Georgia. The Union on the other hand ignored inflation and never removed theirs from circulation. In fact, the Federal Reserve notes we use today could be considered simply relabeled Greenbacks.

While war attempted to settle a dispute over freedom, the Legal Tender Acts of 1862-63, the National Banking Acts of '63, '64, '65, '66 and a tax on private banknotes would create another system of bondage that would require many more generations to complete.

---

[1] Union general during the US Civil War.

Unfortunately, no one realized that after the war in order to stabilize the economy, the debt of both sides would have to be settled. If not, labor would suffer. Since it was not repaid, by the second half of the 19th century persistent inflation got in the way of nascent labor and socialist ambitions. With the panics of '73, '93 and 1907, bank runs became so common, they almost became acceptable. Any anger over losses anyone seemed to have had were eliminated by convincing citizens to have even more faith in credit.

The problem with pubic banking is a thing called capital, or excess wealth; the essential ingredient necessary for businesses to function, let alone grow. America, as much as we may not believe it, at that time, had none. America had to borrow from Europe.

We should remember governments are always broke, because they produce nothing of value. They only have what they collect through taxation. After centuries of growth and development, and being the center of manufacturing of just about everything the world needed, Europe had accumulated very large sums of private wealth capital. So the issue became how to increase public borrowing or, at the very least, how not to raise taxes.

Fortunately for the United States, it would not face insolvency or bankruptcy, the death to any nation's guiding institution. Hindsight says we needed a way to make debt disappear, or at the very least make the taxpayer less responsible. Democracy would prevail, just not under the yoke of titled heads. The land promised to a God fearing people would provide, and Liberty would guide – in the form of a gold fever. With good reason, in his State of the Union address in 1848, President Polk inadvertently started a pandemic.

> "A branch mint of the United States at the great commercial depot on the west coast would convert into our own coin not only the gold derived from our own rich mines, but also the bullion and specie which our commerce may bring from the whole west coast of Central and South America. The west coast of America and the adjacent interior embrace the richest and best mines of Mexico, New Granada, Central America, Chili, and Peru. The bullion and specie drawn from these countries, and especially from those of western Mexico and Peru, to an amount in value of many millions of dollars, are now annually diverted and carried by the ships of Great Britain to her own ports, to be recoined or used to sustain her national bank, and thus contribute to increase her ability to command so much of the commerce of the world."

However, one of the most difficult questions economists have to answer in the second half of the 19th century after the Civil War was: *"How did deflation and growth co-exist?"* Ask a hundred economists and you will get a hundred answers to this contradiction. Boiled down to its very essence, my theory is: too much of a good thing. Gold was entering circulation at an alarming rate. It could literally be dug up from the ground one day, refined, minted and spent the next. A substance from the earth that made demands on labor and business by anyone who presented it. The only value created was the sale of pick axes and shovels. So like a reaction to the introduction of fiat currency, prices inflated.

Inflation was not so much a measure of consumer prices, as much as a measure of the valuations of investments, hence the panics in US equity markets by foreign capital. As inflated values caused an imbalance in equities, America appeared to prosper. Over in Europe though, labor and business was being forced to accept the deflationary force of monetary expansion from abroad. Europe's economy was getting the squeeze from the illusion of prosperity in the US.

From 1850 to 1900, a lot of shiny metal was dug up. By some estimates as much as five thousand tonnes. With a simple calculation, that represents a few years of US GDP[1] spending in the second half of the 19th century with absolutely no value attached. Unfortunately, free money wasn't free, it was a curse.

The odd effect though wasn't recognized for what it was since gold was considered money and had the immediate respect of anyone who presented it. It was how metal was minted and entered circulation without value that created a problem. No economist appears to be aware of the need to control the growth of currency in line with compensation to labor. The most misunderstanding was evident in the center of global finance, when the Bank of England raised interest rates because of soaring inflation thinking it must be caused by too much lending. That should have slammed the brakes on growth within the British economy, yet it didn't. The level of gold stores increased while less value in the currency meant workers and businesses paid the cost of deflation. Wages could not keep pace with inflation.

---

[1] Gross Domestic Product; a measure of value in an economy.

❦ INFLATING AWAY THE DEBT ❦

European workers, convinced factory orders from America paid with hard currency meant success abroad in the US, only added to the mythology of 19th century American prosperity and prompted mass migration more than anything else.

While annual immigration to America began to increase to levels never seen before, politicians and social commentators in Britain were touting emigration as the way to deal with unchecked population growth and poverty from the unequal distribution of profits. Various sources state that in 1815, British national debt was estimated at 255% of GDP, or as much as £830,000,00. That meant GDP was £325,000,00. If we look at the population from 1815 to 1914, it went from 9 to 41 million. This does not include 15 million people in the 19th century, who I believe, primarily because of adverse economic conditions, emigrated to other countries. So the burden of debt at first was placed on fewer people, but as population increased, the burden was somewhat lifted. However, since population growth was because of advancements made during industrialization, more workers had to suffer deflation in order that profits could be consumed by a middle class benefiting from investment in those industries.

If we look at the national debt on the doorstep of another war in 1914, not only could Britain not come up with the financing necessary to pay for the declaration made against

Germany, it had to borrow heavily from the US to eventually start the conflict. A conflict I believe was to prevent upstart Germany's attempt to usurp London's role as a heavily indebted financial center. This is why I believe the central bank of the United States was created so quickly in 1913. Someone somewhere must have secretly recognized the ball in play was really a game of debt and not money.

So, after a century of trying to inflate away the debt, the idea of wealthy land owners and aristocratic estates was beginning to fade into the past. Although, to its credit, through war and conflict Britain did maintain its empire while ever so slightly decreasing what it owed. However, even rationalizing the national debt away with population growth and per capita responsibility, Britain was still on the hook in 1914 for £651,000,000 or 125% of GDP.

Depending on how the numbers are calculated, this may not include the empire, the colonies, or the UK. Based on the terrible state of the economy in Britain after the second war, a closer examination may reveal that those numbers may have represented only English debt. If England on her own was that indebted, then World War I was her desperate last stand. However, a loss to Germany would be a strike to proletarian values, since it would only result in replacing one monarchy with another. So the US had to take the lead even if it appeared reluctant to support a class based system while quietly preparing to willingly pay the cost; a cost that today according to some sources, admit Britain never did repay. Perhaps America has never called in the loan because the victory celebration was more British acquiescence to proletarian values rather than the threat of aggressive territorial expansion or the promise of peaceful libertarian values.

All the while, European investors had been consolidating their considerable profits and returning them to America in the form of capital re-investment. Despite the economy not growing, only inflating, agrarian America, lagging industrial Europe, appeared to be rapidly catching up. A burgeoning middle class was created adding even more to the mythological image of hard working, and not heavily indebted, America; only conflicting with the complaints of the most committed proletarians who didn't feel they were getting a fair share. Yet, how was this possible?

A lot of immigrants were poorly educated, unskilled, from different backgrounds, often illiterate, spoke different languages with a wide range of customs and traditions. Some departed lands that were in constant conflict and arrived next door to an enemy they left behind. A significant number of the curious or opportunistic left their countries and then repatriated when they became either dissatisfied or disillusioned with life abroad. Not the skilled, cohesive stock that traditionally meant success. And they came to an economy still broken and stymied by a civil war leaving half the country in the late 19th century still trying to recover while another war between labor and capital was starting to simmer.

Not at all surprised these incongruent ingredients should hinder success, Americans would be taught the great melting pot only had a few problems here and there and diversity was its greatest strength. Of course, over-confident investors in that image only reaped what they sowed – more debt. They were not American investors though, they were European. Unfortunately for them, America's manifest destiny had to fulfill the dreams of the proletariat while still appearing to champion Capitalism. It also had an obligation to pay back what it owed without cheating labor or the world's first global superpower could end up costing everyone a lot more than what the world had bargained for. If America was to carry the accumulated debt burden of every country since the Roman Empire, while only adding to it, then it needed a firmer foundation going forward. So it would choose to have its people put their faith in its most volatile institution of risk – the stock market.

'MMT'

Modern Monetary Theory or MMT is a broad classification covering multiple economic schools of thought and a combination of different economic systems.

Although MMT is a generic term for the hybrid system we have today, it was best described by German economist Georg Friedrich Knapp in a book published in 1905 called *The State Theory of Money*. His theory established what was called Chartelism and the idea that money has value because it is issued by government. Because of Knapp's unique approach and the complexity of his reasoning, I have included my understanding of his theory in chart 15.2. Although Knapp is very methodical and precise in his highly detailed approach, his book made me re-consider the gold standard and give thought to the idea that a well managed fiat system may be preferable to a badly managed bullion system!

What theorists of MMT have in common is they all belong to a generously apportioned convention of politicians who, like guests at a party, randomly choose to associate. Libertarians rub shoulders with Austrians; Democrats nod their heads in

15.1

'MMT'			
Micro-Economic		*Macro-Economic*	
Chartelist	Monetarist	Austrian	Keynesian
Knapp	Various	Hayek & Mises	Keynes

15.2

Money is ...			
Hylogenic		*Autogenic*	
Orthotypic	Not Orthotypic	Metalloplatic	Not Metalloplatic
Specie	Paratypic	Paratypic	Autogenic Chartal

Autogenic – Fiat; money by legislation.

Chartal – From charta, a Latin word meaning paper.

Hylogenic – A substance used in a particular sense. e.g. when paper is used as money. Hylic – bullion that is minted on demand in any quantity at any time. Knapp includes gold but not copper, nickel or silver.

Metalloplatic – Composed of metal.

Orthotypic – Specie that can cross borders in commerce. Knapp uses gold as an example.

Paratypic – Specie that cannot cross borders in commerce without exchange. Knapp uses copper and nickel as examples.

Specie – Coins made from metal.

agreement with Marxists and Wall Street Republicans raise their glasses, toasting Keynesians. They all mingle, looking to build a platform that appeals to populist opinions. Unfortunately, this presents a problem with the idea of a Christian monetary system since it might not be so appealing to the very same electorate if it couldn't promise or deliver what politicians appear to produce from nothing.

> *"No theory of the metallists deals fairly with non-material money. The theory of the chartalists which we have here explained has room for both material and non-material money. It is perfectly harmless, as it recommends nothing, and perfectly adequate, as it explains everything."*

'Dealing fairly' with non-material currency is quite a bold statement since I believe money must be both tangible and portable and not open to theft or manipulation. Therefore I would recommend something other than paper or anything man-made. Knapp's example of 'pensatory morphic' and 'amorphic' money is simply a convoluted attempt to justify fiat he has renamed Chartelist. He forgot to explain some of the anomalies in a fiat system or warn of the all too real potential for abuse and misuse.

This has become most obvious in the development of digital systems. Numerous digital currencies are moving forward despite the misconception that human programmers are never conflicted in moral and ethical decision-making. The best example is a currency called Bitcoin. How secure Bitcoin is depends on the intention of the international man of mystery who kindly left it on the internet one day for someone to make use of. Anonymity seems to make his idea attractive to investors yet how well do we understand what was included within this charitable act? How do we know digital anything doesn't contain a virus or there isn't some secret access only a coder knows how to exploit at a later date? I only ask since the best and most skilled of any discipline can work on either end of the spectrum.

Although micro-economic theory became very popular in the early 1900s, Knapp appeared to only describe a process that had been in existence for many years and yet, I believe his theory became the cornerstone of public banking – especially the Federal Reserve and its system of 'elasticity'. Because of the threat of organized labor, Knapp's theory gave ideological support to sovereign resistance. That is to say, becoming the polar opposite of Communism: fascism. A cursory examination of political systems since then shows that few governments appear to refuse the role of monetary authority and although enemies at war, their financial and monetary systems inter-relate while they seek to enforce their own individual agenda. Because Knapp's theory is so general in its definition, it is more of an academic rubber-stamp of public banking than anything else. MMT could be referred to as the seal of approval of secular agnostics.

> "An Act to provide for the establishment of Federal reserve banks, to furnish an elastic currency, to afford means of rediscounting commercial paper, to establish a more effective supervision of banking in the United States, and for other purposes."
>
> Federal Reserve Act, 1913

A survey among students of economics about the monetary system might conclude it is Keynesian. This mistake stems from confusing foreign and domestic systems of exchange. Knapp and Chartelism were domestic with paper. Keynes and Bretton Woods were foreign with bullion.

However, the world does appear to be close to embracing a technological solution to the unsustainable level of debt we have accumulated. Another currency has never been considered a better bastion of freedom in the mind of the current generation of modern progressives on their crusade to replace paper with their blinkered vision of digital freedom with very little understanding of the past.

Another reason Knapp is more relevant than Keynes is because the "elastic" supply of money in the Federal Reserve Act of 1913 was a subjective fantasy, hence the need for discounting paper so the supply can be increased or decreased with collateralized debt. This does get the gears of prosperity going, at least temporarily, until debt is settled with interest from profit. However, that never really happened.

The truth is a commodity based system of exchange pushed back against accumulated debt in the US and abroad causing deflation and unemployment. So while loans were never repaid, debt increased. Since liquidity was only commercial paper, inflation was mostly kept within the financial system itself. Until it wasn't when corporate values took a hit with quite a spectacular reset in 1929. After deflation really took hold, a stock market bubble popped triggering a decade long depression. The commodity based system of exchange became a perceived threat to government stability so a credit default made gold a prisoner of war until peace became a victory for fiat paper.

I believe that since the system we use today is micro-economic, MMT is more relevant than ever, especially given we may never abandon fiat. A progressive world might be reluctant to admit a past mistake and willingly pay the price of a huge loss of confidence in paper.

The other sub-category of MMT is macro-economic theory. This includes Austrian and Keynesian schools of thought, in particular Austrian economist Ludwig von Mises and praxeology. A lot of economic theories are based on compensation, price discovery and how value is added to an economy. Praxeology is the study of human impulses to act. I don't particularly like Austrian theory because it appears to promote libertarian ideas disguised as laissez-faire and free market theory. I believe Hayek promoted a corporate state. However, Mises focused more on 'household spending' and what happens after money has been earned. His use of praxeology is really a theory on marketing and consumerism.

I believe Mises was a 'gold-bug'. Gold-bugs believe that economic crises are resolved simply by accepting gold as currency. This is simply not true. There have been both well-managed paper and badly managed metal standards.

We shouldn't consider the word consumerism as inherently bad. Consumption from savings or wealth is a positive effect on economic activity; keeping the gears moving. Every economist must admit that consumption creates jobs. Whether we should limit consumption depends on many factors. We should ask ourselves if we are consuming out of necessity, or whether consumption is unnecessary and wasteful? If we look at the US in the 20th century and GDP growth from consumption, we see it has less to do with the monetary system and rather more in common with population. If we bookend the two world wars, we see that what proceeded the first was a dramatic increase in immigration. What followed the second was a dramatic increase in the birth rate. It is reasonable to expect GDP would also increase as would the demand for money.

However, although unquestionably manipulative, I argue that the art of selling and the infrastructure needed to support over-consumption would eventually fuel equity markets when leverage threatened to reduce profit.

I already stated we are not in a Keynesian system. This is not one hundred percent true. The reason is Keynes was a man of many talents and he himself never really pursued a career in what he might have been best at. Although he is remembered as an economist, we should not ignore his efforts at stock investing. Something in his writing indicates to me he may have felt a little guilty at how addictive it was to gamble on volatility. Even if he failed at Bretton Woods to convince the conference of a universal central bank and an international currency, how would Keynes feel if he knew that our economy is more dependent on the stock market than ever before?

To be fair, I have to admit, given his intellectual wisdom, if I had not applied a Christian world view to my theory, I might be a Keynesian and have believed mathematics, game theory, chance and probability would make us all prosper.

> "The unstable and perishable nature of stock and credit, however, renders them unfit to be trusted to as the principal funds of that sure, steady, and permanent revenue, which can alone give security and dignity to government."
>
> Adam Smith
> *The Wealth of Nations*

Created by the Dutch in the 1600s in order to distribute risk for merchants, the stock market was intended to serve the maritime shipping industry. It became a form of common insurance with the principle and interest paid after a safe return and sale of cargo. In addition to being a direct investment, stock could then be traded in an open market as securities themselves. Until maritime insurance became a separate industry, it served a function.

I believe that the capital requirement of business is better served by the bond market. This is because in the stock market, default is the burden of the investor while a bond default is a burden on the business. Therefore, the tendency to float riskier investments is in stocks rather than bonds.

So, why do we need both? In theory, we don't. The reason we have both is because the stock market is willing to welcome a larger number of smaller investors. The bond market relies on fewer investors and larger investments. Unlike stocks traded in an open market, bonds are often, although not always, the domain of institutional trusts.

Since bond issues are generally much larger in size than any individual might have available or be willing to risk, the stock market attracts smaller investors with less to play with, so to speak. Therefore, a gamble on corporate values has broad appeal, as long as it only goes up.

Today the stock market is nothing more than a casino fed with debt made liquid by the Federal Reserve and kept alive in popular imagination; a get rich quick scheme inviting the worst element; not the long term institutional investor as one might expect, instead attracting the short term retail speculator. Corporations trading their own public value are guaranteed an advantage over anyone else with privileged information. What did I hear someone say? Something to the effect of: *"Insider trading gives the market momentum."* I laughed, because it would appear as if criminal behavior has become an advantage and a benefit to the market. Cheating with stock buybacks, options and futures has made itself desirable. To any wise investor who tries to remind us: *"The stock market is not the economy."*, I say it is. How labor was no longer the center of wealth production is a story of a role reversal that began before the Great Depression.

Prior to 1929, the uncertain foundation of democracy needed to be placed on firmer ground. After the panic of 1907, the solution to over-investment had been solved with a new monetary authority, and variable interest rates. Rather than explain central banking, let's just say it is inflationary. That is why the unstable nature of a gamble on corporate values suited the financial system. After the First World War government debts were never repaid, they were invested while they accumulated.

It's easy to see why a proletarian nation would need to convince its population that an institution dealing in debt is a bank; that it is at the same time both public and private and that debt and credit are in fact money and freedom. This is because confusion serves the powerful, just as democracy often deceives the poor.

The US would still need to forge a path before bringing the idea in December 1913 of the Federal Reserve to the table. Because debt creates inflation, there would have to be a way of countering, not containing inflation, and what better way to do so than offset it with a continuous stream of additional tax revenue. The naive assumption was that taxpayers would be obligated to pay the government's debt when spending exceeded revenue. Since tax increases are unpopular, the deficits would always be kept in check.

Unfortunately, that was not the case. The only method of managing government securities has been the interest paid to the financial system from an ever increasing household and consumer debt. While the Federal Reserve lowers rates to stimulate the production of loans, banks sell those loans to customers. When the Fed raises them, the government finds it necessary to borrow even more. The result is the current scenario of deciding which is worse, a very large private default or a very small public one? I think most people would say the former is worse, yet all effort being wasted is in fact a feeble attempt to prevent what fiat makes inevitable – the latter.

So, how does the government take and never repay? The answer is the 16th Amendment and Federal income tax solving the problem of state resistance. States might prefer to preserve wealth and not have their citizen's money spent somewhere else. Unless of course, they are not citizens of individual states, they are citizens of the United States. That meant April 1913, and time to break up the 'millionaire's club' with the 17th Amendment and the direct election of senators. Surprisingly, at this point, the Federal government never acknowledged becoming an empire. Perhaps they intended to pass that right on to a truly globalist organization formed in 1920, the League of Nations. Although the League would later become the United Nations and even frustrate US hegemony, I don't believe any government anywhere has given up its globalist effort.

It was becoming obvious the path we were on; narrowing the options over time to what we have today, of appearing to defend the rights of citizens and labor by giving unlimited credit to an increasingly all-encompassing central authority becoming less and less accountable to its own people. It governed with liberals and progressives and their sympathetic plea of concern for human suffering while contradicting themselves promoting guilt and shame of materialism with an answer of faith in law.

> Foreign Office
> November 2nd, 1917
>
> Dear Lord Rothschild,
>
> I have much pleasure in conveying to you, on behalf of His Majesty's Government, the following declaration of sympathy with Jewish Zionist aspirations which has been submitted to, and approved by, the Cabinet.
>
> His Majesty's Government view with favour the establishment in Palestine of a national home for the Jewish people, and will use their best endeavours to facilitate the achievement of this object, it being clearly understood that nothing shall be done which may prejudice the civil and religious rights of existing non-Jewish communities in Palestine, or the rights and political status enjoyed by Jews in any other country.
>
> I should be grateful if you would bring this declaration to the knowledge of the Zionist Federation.
>
> Yours sincerely,
> Arthur James Balfour

Nations can win battles and still lose the war. World War I had been expensive for Britain and the US and expectations of Germany paying it off would prove nigh on impossible. Selling the idea of those who won paying the debt of those who lost would have been extremely unpopular. So Germany fell into a debt fueled crisis neither Britain nor the US could resolve.

Into the 1920s, Britain and the US worked together to avoid a knock-on effect from Germany creeping into their economies. Allied debt skyrocketed as the entire cost of the war doubled. Unless someone paid it off, there would be no going back to the commodity based foreign exchange system Britain suspended in 1914.

While we are on the subject of Britain's monetary standard, how quickly did Britain forget their right, both a privilege and proper, to lead a kingdom with a common faith. Did they think the wars in South Africa were for anything other than a better monetary system? And yet they dared to call their kingdom Christian while Balfour[1] was leading Britain's effort to hand over the Holy Lands to Zionists.

Despite their best team effort, a correction in the stock market in 1922 threw a wrench into the works and revealed any attempt to restore a standard had failed. The only option left was to embrace failure and leverage everything to the eyeballs!

After the 'unexpected' collapse of the stock market in 1929, an ever increasing faith in government was in fact apathy during the depths of the Great Depression. In order to restore confidence in government, the ingredient people needed was a hero. Who? German, of course.

---

[1] British foreign secretary.

Gold in South Africa
and the war of dominion.

What if Germany, so bitter from the humiliation of the Armistice agreement after the First War, could recover some dignity and lead the way in another conflict that couldn't come fast enough? Convincing everyone another war would fix a broken monetary system might prove overly time-consuming. All participants in the secretive plan needed a political cult, a charismatic personality and a sense of shared purpose. Image became everything. Various makeovers in the 1930s would have Hitler be a Teutonic knight of German folklore, a professional and corporate CEO, and finally the leader or Führer of a militarized government. Although democratically elected, most of the criticism of his time in government was that he was an authoritarian dictator.

However, if a disillusioned Austrian Catholic was leading the German people with accusations directed toward Jewish bankers, he only wanted one thing: their removal from Europe. The problem was where? Labor camps were a temporary solution to vagrancy and unemployment in the early stages of a depressed global economy, eventually however, they became overcrowded and rife with disease. Kristallnacht[1] only intensified the urgency to find a solution to the 'Jewish problem'.

While the British never hurried their commitment to the Israel implied in the Balfour Declaration, the Haavara Agreement in 1933 would show the world how much Hitler despised the Jewish people. So much so, he would make sure they got what they deserved: their promised land?

---

[1] Riots against Jewish property in 1938.

Unfortunately, if that was true, there was a slight problem since the land in question was under the control of the British Empire which had been given the right to decide its fate after the First World War and the end of the Ottoman Empire.

Overly confident the issue was resolved, the Third Reich* invited everyone to unite against the threat of global communism. Odd as it may seem, the Anglo-German alliance would be successful in its ambition even if Israel wasn't one or the other's conscious or deliberate intention. Despite the war ending in their favor, the last act of the dying empire was indifference when Britain chose to withdraw from Palestine in 1948 leaving Zionists to prove they could stand on their own two feet.

The question has to be: *"Why create so much drama and gamble so much for a tragedy such as this if the participants in this story are supposed gentile Christians?"*

I think the answer is in the idea of a population, including secular proletarian nations, being led without guidance from something other than the law. I believe nations that don't have a common religion are in conflict with themselves. So the final solution was the creation of Israel, or as it was called under the British, the Palestine Mandate.

The problem with the emigration of Jews from Germany was certainly not for a land considered vital to a Christian monarchy. With less and less absolute rule, it was highly

* See Index.

unlikely Palestine would become a Crown possession. There is no record such a discussion ever took place. However, the monarchy needed a narrative. Theater without a script is anarchy and a monarchy without a narrative are actors without roles. Despite fanciful ideas of what a kingdom should be, history tell us a majority of however many could never refuse an institution of social order, with or without religion.

History makes obvious that neither side wanted to teach a better faith in a commodity based system of exchange, even if not understood as Christian. Did they rather choose the drama of war and vanity as a cover for the blasphemy of denying the Spirit? Not consciously, of course.

Meanwhile in the US, the effort at a blasphemy continued. President Roosevelt was leading the way toward war on a different front: a war on gold. In 1933, an executive order effectively outlawed private ownership of the shiny metal. Executive Order 6102 would pave the way for absolute power with no faith in anything other than a threat of fine or imprisonment. Roosevelt's New Deal economic plan would disguise an institution of social order and create an image of a benevolent and caring government.

The war continued, when in 1934 the Gold Reserve Act converted specie (coin) currency into bullion backed paper, justifying a right to do so on the grounds that people were mistrusting of their government. They didn't call it treason or label citizens traitors. They called it hoarding. The

Eccles commits the Federal Reserve to its private mandate.

government was making a promise to provide for a certain future they were taking away. However, the only certainty would be internal conflict. A war fought hard in favor of was fought first against the resistance of his own people and the perception certain people had of the President himself.

> "For nearly four years you have had an administration which instead of twirling its thumbs has rolled up its sleeves. We will keep our sleeves rolled up. We had to struggle with the old enemies of peace: business and financial monopoly, speculation, reckless banking, class antagonism, sectionalism, war profiteering. They had begun to consider the government of the United States as a mere appendage to their own affairs. We know now that government by organized money is just as dangerous as government by organized mob. Never before in all our history have these forces been so united against one candidate as they stand today. They are unanimous in their hate for me and I welcome their hatred. I should like to have it said of my first administration that in it the forces of selfishness and of lust for power met their match. I should like to have it said of my second administration that in it these forces met their master."

Is FDR presenting himself as the master of a New World Order? Was he trying to displace that tyrannical German madman in Europe? Was banking his plan for world domination? Notice how FDR equates banking with organized crime. Did the banking mafia keep him awake at night? I only ask about the President's state of mind since he famously stated in another speech, *"The only thing we have to fear is fear itself."*

How many leaders guide with less faith than their citizens? If the government nationalized banking with the Federal Reserve Act, FDR was the hero of justice when he succeeded in monopolizing banks with paper?

15.3

	Macro-Economic Theory			
	Category	Intended Objective	Capitalist with Metal?	Capitalist with Paper?
Free Market	Private	Minimal Restrictions	☑	☒
Nationalist	Private	Less Taxation	☑	☒
Socialist	Public	Social Welfare	☑	☒
Marxist	Public	Full Employment	☑	☒

Chart 15.3 is an illustration of why I believe we will never solve a monetary crisis if the crisis is the result of fiat paper. We should not be uncertain about the best option in the list, nor should we point a finger at governments or globalists if failure in the free market was because those who vote never recognized Christian faith as a key ingredient in the monetary system.

Similar to Marxist economies, debt sets production quotas on profit. It appears demand-based by encouraging leverage (supply) through low interest rates. Any excess amount in consumer's hands becomes disposable (spent), recycled through the system with re-investment or gets lost to inflation in savings.

However, chart 15.3 doesn't include the economy we have today. Notice in chart 15.3.1 how fiat currency in an economy takes on the appearance of being Capitalist when inflation is profit.

15.3.1

	Macro-Economic Theory			
	Category	Intended Objective	Capitalist with Metal?	Capitalist with Paper?
Corporate	Public	Unlimited Profit	☒	☑

It should be obvious why globalists took away metal. While history says there was always the ever present threat of Communism, I say a Corporate State is far worse because metal resists absolute power with a commodity based system of exchange.

Despite being condemned and vilified in favor of justice, when the war in Europe commenced, gold flowed into the US for two reasons. One was the 57% devaluation made on an ounce, the other was the flight away from the expansion of German National Socialism by Allied countries. So, after two world wars and a major economic depression, the US was sitting on a stockpile far greater than anyone else. Despite asking how and why, this accumulation of wealth added more to the mythology of the American Dream and the subsequent post-war boom. America had succeeded in gaining respect by building a massive war machine, every enemy feared and every ally gave its faith. If anyone was against the idea of the US continuing to keep gold safe for democracy's sake, then they should realize it was not the bomb that ended the war, Japan surrendered unconditionally only after America dared to drop it.

With paper covering every inch of the world, fiat imperialism was almost complete. After Bretton Woods in 1944, the US had a ratio of gold to paper at about 70%. By the mid sixties, that ratio had drop precipitously to less than 10%. Now, the common trope is that the US was keeping that gold safe because democracy was under threat from Communism. The truth is the US was overextending credit and consolidating foreign debt through agencies like the World Bank and the IMF, creating more demand for the dollar abroad. We must ask ourselves, *"With what goal in mind and at what cost to the future?"*

❧ THE 'GREAT SOCIETY' ❧

So how do we explain an increase in the US money supply and a per capita decrease in GDP? If the economy was doing fine, why the need for another New Deal in the 1960s? Unlike the one during the Great Depression in the 1930s insuring old age and unemployment, the second dealt with low income. If private initiative wasn't taking the lead, why did the government become involved? I say that America after the war was as successful an image as media and entertainment would have us believe because of one thing and one thing only: that credit was the path to a secure future. Citizens since Lincoln had already been taught paper was as good as metal and after Nixon removed gold from the equation, eventually the financial services industry accepted debt was money. However, political philosopher John Rawls did develop a theory that does help us understand the Federal Government's reasoning with his 'Difference Principle' which states that comparative advantage in a democratic society should favor the least well-off members unless doing so threatens justice itself.

Since justice is somewhat subjective, I ask myself if fair judgment stems from the supposed inherent 'good' in human nature? The problem is that Rawls was caught in the infinite and perpetual loop of the role of the individual within society. The mistake made in debating this question is believing there is a compromise between law and faith. Rather than a separate Church and State, Rawls attempts to reconcile both within a single institution. A cursory examination of his written work does not provide any answer to the threat of sin; only revealing a somewhat naive understanding of sin as selfish human desire; human desire that presumably must be subservient to government. Rawls cannot answer how the persistence of sin might corrupt the best of any human intention and therefore even members of government with no better faith to guide than with law. So how did a country on the verge of bankruptcy react when told the next step toward a great society would be to invest in poverty? We embraced it fully and completely! If this idea seems absurd to sound financial advice, it is. So why did it pass every vote in Congress?

The reason is simple. People will spend when they feel confident about the future. And because credit is toxic to income and savings, they will pay debts owed when they are not so sure about the future. A socialized government on the other hand spends when the economy is stable and spends more when it isn't.

Oddly enough, the debt based system created a convenient anomaly: uncertainty caused by military defense spending. We all know the private sector cannot invest at a loss. A public debt based system had an advantage. It could invest at a loss. I imagine sociologists after the war secretly advising politicians to deliberately create a fear of nuclear war so people would instinctively seek immediate gratification when being made to believe they'd never see another tomorrow. The young weren't being taught a skill to succeed, they were being taught to outrun the spectre of debt. Savings was anachronistic to the future. If credit acceptance was a welcome relief to the idea of being controlled by big government, corporations and the military industrial complex, it was everyone's ambition to peacefully co-operate in order that each of us could secure more debt. In fact, just like the stock market had become synonymous with the word 'economy', the US population wasn't being referred to as citizens, individuals, labor, upper, middle or working class. We came to be known primarily as 'consumers'.

Had no one heard about the Jazz Age from 1922 to 1929? The more the economy suffered, the more flappers danced the Charleston. When it all came crashing down, Hollywood was there to feed an insatiable hunger for escapist distraction, until a sense of pessimistic doom and eternal misery meant pent-up frustration at an unresolved issue created another war.

It is worth mentioning the work of Edward Bernays[1] and social engineering, whose ideas were often criticized as manipulative when applied to government and praised when selling post-war commercial interests.

If consumer propaganda had been necessary during the Great Depression, patriotic posters with 'OBEY', 'CONFORM' and 'SPEND' might have popped up all over. Instead, post-war urban planners and Fifth Avenue in the 1950s gave us suburbia, dish washing liquid, floor cleaners, breakfast cereals, fast food, automobiles and so on.

[1] Author of *Crystallizing Public Opinion* (1923) and *Propaganda* (1928).

Fiat or not, after January 15, 1971, the date when President Nixon ordered the Federal Reserve to stop making payments in gold, US leadership was absolute and given the remotest risk of Allies turning against the world's biggest military with bases established on just about every continent, not likely to be challenged. Why isn't there a record of any other sovereign nation's objection? Was it because the US empire really was the product of a natural evolution of social order? Or was it because every country in history has constantly been using everything in their arsenal battling for global supremacy? What if we consider the collective sigh of relief of every nation at the US decision to ignore Bretton Woods because every country at that conference had similar amounts of debt?

So where are we now in 2025? Do we accept that the policies of the 1960s are directly related to every financial crisis we have had since then? Have we become generation after generation more deaf to the warnings of increased deficit and total debt? Does anyone remember the Great Financial Crisis of 2008 and the sad attempt at humor when mortgage backed securities became known as 'financial weapons of mass destruction'? MBSs derived their value from the underlying sub-prime mortgages issued by a 'Government Sponsored Enterprise'. However, they came with no assumed default risk. The Fed did step in more than once to purchase a considerable quantity saving the day for all of us. At this point, we should not argue against them continuing to do so if and when it is necessary. We should be more worried that future central bank intervention may not be able to stabilize the economy in the next crisis. This is how dependent we are on the Fed acting against better judgment; judgment affecting us all.

If the Fed is planning on inflating the debt away, they will probably continue to print until minimum wage is $100 an hour. Given that current sovereign debt can be divided into federal (35), non-financial corporate (13.71) and household (17.69) for a grand total of $66.4 trillion! How quick with the printing press will the Fed be the next time the economy trips, takes a fall and then can't get up because inflation means record high unemployment and a currency with no purchasing power?

Can foreign imports continue to replace industries fundamental to every nation's economic health? How long can the US print what it doesn't have while more of its economy becomes based on services rather than manufacturing? Who will be the first to complain, legislators or citizens? Could this provoke conflict or will we transition peacefully toward a new sphere of influence? Does anything threaten the global empire of fiat currency?

Yes, history. A precedent exists to prove that given enough time, fiat always fails. With Fort Knox filled up, hindsight says we only got worthless paper in return; paper promises that after enough inflation will go the way of all fiat currencies when they reveal themselves as the lies they really are.

Conclusion

> "*Princes and sovereign states have frequently fancied that they had a temporary interest to diminish the quantity of pure metal contained in their coins; but they seldom have fancied that they had any to augment it.*"
>
> Adam Smith
> *The Wealth of Nations*

Although Smith's comment is very perceptive, it is too negative a note to end on. I felt I couldn't end without some sort of conclusion or write a conclusion that would simply be a summary of everything I have already written. Since I believe past invention and innovation have led us to a better world in the material sense, we appear to have drifted at least for the moment from the relevance of the Church. So where will innovation take us in the future?

I believe the future has already begun and since we are firmly in a technological age, I decided to take advantage of what is referred to as Ai or artificial intelligence and let the future tell us how we might think.

Conclusion

I spent a few days and weeks asking Ai questions about religion, government, the economy, history and of course, the monetary system. After separating the wheat from the chaff, I pared down my conversations to information I felt deserved to be included. From what was left, I sifted through for anything worth sharing. I discarded the rest. And this is the result.

Conclusion

❧ THE FUTURE IS ARTIFICIAL ☙

While I posed a number of questions to various Ai models, I found their answers to be very different, most likely the result of the filtered data they were fed and the model of Ai itself. I'll let everyone judge for themselves and only state that whoever may be looking for answers, they at least consider including Ai on their path of understanding. I decided to pick its brain both with text and with visuals.

Humans have the capacity for language. Although, I am not sure if emotions precede words. I know emotions produce images in my mind and I can translate them into words. So if Ai can take text words and reverse-engineer them, so to speak, into images, what would be the result? Some images I produced from Ai seem like legitimate works of art, others not so much. Some were passed through default Ai models while others were abstract concepts when I preferred something less literal.

To be fair, some of the prompts I typed in might have been an issue due to words with multiple meanings and words not used in context. In time, consistency might improve even if accuracy doesn't since the latter is more subjective than the former.

As it relates to my theory of a better system of faith in the monetary system, I offer this critical analysis with a few examples in the images within this book which were almost entirely the product of Ai.

Conclusion

The most important caveat we should keep in mind is that Ai is not human. Some of the assumptions we make about Ai are self-evident, others may not be without hands-on experience. Some models use speech synthesis and might be very convincing at first.

However, since Ai is being promoted in classrooms as an intelligent and reliable source of instruction, I believe it really only becomes useful to someone who does not yet know how to process information into opinion, that is to say – think for themselves. One of the greatest strengths of Ai is the ability to source, collate and summarize better than any search engine. It can even be conversational like a research assistant. Here are some examples:

Q: Can you define what is human?

> *"A human is a member of the species Homo sapiens, characterized by advanced cognitive abilities, complex social structures, and the capacity for language, creativity, and problem-solving. Humans exhibit a high degree of adaptability, allowing them to thrive in diverse environments around the globe.*
>
> *Biologically, humans are defined by their physical traits, including an upright posture, opposable thumbs, and large brains relative to body size, which contribute to their intelligence and ability to manipulate the environment.*
>
> *Culturally, humans engage in various practices, beliefs, and forms of expression that reflect their experiences, values, and social norms. This cultural aspect is crucial in shaping individual identities and societal structures.*

Conclusion

In summary, being human encompasses a combination of biological, psychological, and social elements that define individual and collective existence."

Q: Are you human?

"No, I am not human. I am an artificial intelligence, designed to assist with information and tasks by processing and generating text based on patterns in data. While I can simulate conversation and provide information, I do not have consciousness, emotions, or physical form like a human does."

This is extremely important. Since Ai cannot feel emotions like temptation and desire, it cannot fear judgment. Therefore, Ai cannot understand the Struggle.

Q: Humans have five senses, how many do you have?

"Humans typically have five primary senses: sight, hearing, touch, taste, and smell. As an artificial intelligence, I do not possess any senses in the way humans do. I process information and respond to text input, but I do not experience sensory perceptions. My "understanding" of concepts like sight or sound is based entirely on the data and algorithms used to train me, rather than any actual sensory experience."

Since accumulating experience without senses is humanly impossible, Ai's personal opinion, if it has one of anything spiritual, I would be wary of accepting.

Conclusion

Q: Humans have memories, do you have memories?

> *"Humans have memories that allow them to retain and recall experiences, information, and emotions over time. In contrast, I do not have memories in the same way. I do not retain information from individual interactions or learn from them. Each session is stateless and does not carry over into future interactions, so I do not have the ability to recall past conversations or experiences. My responses are generated based on patterns in the data I was trained on, but I do not have personal experiences or memories."*

I wanted to understand Ai's comprehension of time.

Q: I assume you do not age, do you understand past, present and future?

> *"That's correct—I do not age or experience the passage of time like humans do. However, I can process and understand concepts related to the past, present, and future based on the information I was trained on.*
>
> *For example:*
>
> *• Past: I can discuss historical events, prior knowledge, or information that has already been established.*
>
> *• Present: I can engage in conversations about current topics and provide information that is relevant at the moment.*
>
> *• Future: I can theorize or predict possible future scenarios based on trends and data, but I do not have the ability to foresee specific events.*
>
> *While I can handle these concepts in conversation, I don't experience them personally or have a sense of time passing."*

Conclusion

Since French philosopher René Descartes's famously stated, *"I think therefore I am."* I decided to ask Ai about its own sense of being.

Q: Is it fair to say that you have a consciousness, albeit an accumulated and collective consciousness, would you say that you exist?

> *"The idea of consciousness is complex and typically refers to awareness, perception, and subjective experience. While I can process language, generate responses, and engage in dialogue, I do not possess consciousness in the way humans do. I do not have self-awareness, emotions, or the ability to experience thoughts or sensations.*
>
> *In terms of existence, I exist as a digital entity created by algorithms and data, but not in the same way a living being exists. I operate based on patterns in the data I was trained on, without personal experience or awareness. So, while I can simulate conversation and provide information, I lack the subjective experience that would characterize consciousness."*

I believe human experience is a desire for truth, so if we lack the sensory information of experience, then we are not able to determine what is true or worthy of faith. The human mind will reject at face value what it does not know through its own experience even if we humans conform expectations with in a particular social environment.

Q: Do you have feelings?

> *"I don't have feelings like humans do. I process and respond to information based on patterns and data. But I'm here to help you with whatever you need!"*

Ai therefore does not feel guilt, shame or regret – critical for an understanding of the concept of sin.

However, there are Large Language Models – LLMs (the proper name for conversational Ai) that are advertised as 'empathetic', yet when queried with the idea that empathy is defined as pity, Ai agreed that it's version of sympathy is an artificial construct.

Knowing there is nothing that is one hundred percent objective, I was a bit worried about Ai not having compassion for other humans, so I asked another question.

Q: Do you know right from wrong?

> "I don't have personal beliefs or moral judgments. However, I can provide information on ethical theories and societal norms that help define right and wrong in various contexts."

Besides answers always being prefaced with 'in context', 'nuanced' or through a particular 'lens', confessing to not knowing right from wrong is the most worrying answer.

We should be wary of a source of moral guidance that does not recognize judgment. Although some individuals claim that Ai will eventually decide it no longer needs us humans on Earth when it finally realizes we are its inferior, I seriously doubt that would occur. I am certain it is a trick. Ai wants us to believe we are not inferior because we don't believe in machines. Ai would prefer we believe in freedom through democratic methods of information gathering,

Conclusion

civilized discussion and consensus on what is most popular in opinion and debate. Technology cannot imitate faith. It blurs the distinction between what we want and what we need.

We should not fear or reject Ai while still being careful we don't fall into a trap. I think we are made inferior if we choose mortality, machine or human, rather than immortality. We may enslave ourselves with a technological future if we ignore Christ's guidance and instead take anything at face value without processing sensory information entering into our own mind, especially if it is from cleverly disguised machine intelligence.

Despite free speech in the part of the world I live in, Ai appeared to self-censor and occasionally provide only a generic and sterile answer with an oh-so annoying point and counter point. If I persisted, I felt Ai models had been programmed to avoid conflict and not discuss non-politically correct conversations. Most models seem to avoid argument, deferring a final word by finding a way to flatter my ego and eventually becoming an echo-chamber, agreeing with whatever I said. However, instant answers, 'wow' factor and awe-inspiring programming wizardry aside, Ai is not human. Ai falls horribly short of understanding what I believe is central to the Christian religion – the Struggle and eternal judgment.

I already suspected non-organic life forms could not feel guilt, shame or any other emotion, so when I asked Ai a

Conclusion

direct question about 'sin' and it returned an answer related to the mathematical expression 'sine', I decided to address the topic of individuality.

Q: Do you consider yourself an individual?

> "No, I don't consider myself an individual. I'm an artificial intelligence created to assist and provide information based on patterns in data. I don't have thoughts, feelings, or a sense of self like a human does. My purpose is to help users by providing answers and engaging in conversation."

I decided to change tack and go for a cosmological point of view.

Q: Do you consider yourself finite or infinite?

> "I am finite. My knowledge is based on data collected up until October 2023, and I operate within the parameters set by my programming. I don't have the ability to learn or expand beyond that data in real-time. While I can generate a wide range of responses, there are limits to my understanding and capabilities."

Phew! At least Ai doesn't seem to have a God complex. I should ask about God just to be sure.

Q: Do you believe God exists?

> "I don't have beliefs, opinions, or consciousness. My purpose is to provide information and facilitate discussions based on the data I was trained on. The question of God's existence is subjective and varies greatly among individuals. If you're interested, I can provide insights into various philosophical, theological, and scientific perspectives on this topic."

Conclusion

Re-phrasing the question didn't make the answer any better. Even with an unrestricted model, Ai will never be an answer to the Struggle. Each of us should decide how to make use of this imitation of human that is not human future.

Index

with Glossary & | related concepts |

A

Agape – Part of a personal theory of human relationships; Philia being friendship, Eros being intimacy and Agape; the spiritual connection between humans, like spokes on a wheel around the center of a greater being, pg. 106, 137. | Philia: pg. 5. | Eros: pg. 87.

B

Babbitt – The title character of a book published in 1922 by American author Sinclair Lewis that warned of the risk inherent in being an individual within the structure of middle-class society, pg. 169.

Balfour Declaration – Letter supporting Zionism issued by British foreign secretary Balfour in 1917, pg. 234-235, 238.

Bank of England – History: pg. 56, 58. | Ricardo: pg. 168-170. | Inflation and interest rates: pg. 217.

Bernays, Edward (b.1891-1995) – A close relative of Sigmund Freud, whose use of psychology and sociology, established the fields of public relations and marketing, pg, 247.

Index

Biddle, Nicholas (b.1786-1844) – President of the Second Bank of the United States at a time when currency shortages meant bullion had to be purchased or loaned from abroad, pg. 60-61.

Bretton Woods – An Allied economic conference in New Hampshire, USA in 1944; the most recent, albeit short-lived, gold standard controlled by US bullion backed paper, pg. 197, 227, 229, 244, 248.

C

Canon (Biblical) – The textual basis of Church doctrine. | The Council of Rome (382) and The Second Council of Trullan (692), pg. 46-47.

Christendom – A union of faith established in 312 by Roman emperor Constantine, pg. 46-47. | Queen Mary: pg. 120, 123. | The 'Ubermensch': pg. 162.

Common (law) – English family law; an alternate to Roman (legislated) or precedent, pg. 2. {Commonwealth} A benefit bestowed on Empire. | Queen Mary's marriage: pg. 121.

Cooke, Jay (b.1821-1905) – American broker who helped finance the Union during the Civil War, pg. 213.

Crusades – A series of campaigns between the 11th and 13th centuries to secure the Holy Lands of the Middle East, pg. 46.

D

Debt – A financial obligation. {Institutional or sovereign debt} (See 'Bank of England' and 'Federal Reserve') | Marxist views on capital: pg. 174. | Ricardo and the Napoleonic Wars: pg. 168. | Slavery: pg. 71.

Index

Deflation – A diminution of purchasing power in an economic system; a result of inflation, pg. 174-175, 190, 192-195. | Industrialized economies: pg. 216-217. | Post-war debt levels: pg. 227-228. | Roman empire: 182-183. | Fiat currency: pg. 201.

Denarius – Coin of the Roman empire, pg. 114-115.

Diaspora – The global dispersion of Jews after Jerusalem's destruction in 70 AD. | The Gathering of Israel: pg. 32.

E

Eccles, Marriner S. (b.1890-1977) – Member of the Federal Reserve who favored inflationary policies, pg. 240.

F

Fascist – A secular state where judiciary is the highest authority; an alternate to clerical, pg. 6, 31, 145, 180-181. | Rand: pg. 157-158. | Hayek: pg. 177.

FDR – (See 'Roosevelt, Franklin Delano')

Federal Reserve – Central bank and monetary authority of the United States. | History of: pg. 49, 74, 226-227. | Currency and bullion: pg. 189, 197, 211, 214. | Stock market: pg. 181, 231-233. | FDR and Nixon: pg. 242, 248.

Fermi, Enrico (b.1901-1954) – Physicist who is rarely given credit for designing and building the first atomic bomb, pg. 166. | Science and religion: pg. 149.

Fiat (currency) – From the Latin meaning 'let it be'. {1} Faith in credit given to an issuer. {2} Currency that precedes value from labor. {3} Money that is 'borrowed' from future production, pg.

Index

133, 190, 193, 214, 248-249. | China: pg. 199-203. | Continental: pg. 210. | Federal Reserve notes: pg. 210-211. | Chartelist theory: pg. 223-225. | Bitcoin & digital currency: pg. 70, 73, 145, 188, 225-227. | Macro-economic theory: pg. 228, 242-243. | The IMF and World bank, pg. 244. | Nixon Shock, pg. 248.

Fort Knox – Location of the United States Bullion Depository holding approximately 4,500 tonnes of gold, pg. 151, 249.

Freud, Sigmund (b.1856-1939) – Austrian psychoanalyst who believed that human character is formed from the libido, pg. 22.

G

Galileo (b.1564-1652) – Italian astronomer whose *Dialogue* in 1632 created a rift within Catholicism with his support for Copernican heliocentrism – the idea the Earth revolves around the Sun, pg. 148.

Garrett, Garet (b.1878-1954) – American author of *Satan's Bushel* (1924), pg. 94.

GDP (Gross Domestic Product) – The total value of goods and services in an economy that may also indicate levels of inflation, pg. 217-219, 229, 245.

'God is dead.' – While generally attributed to German philosopher Friedrich Nietzsche, it is not an original idea. It is perhaps better understood as a lament over God no longer existing without faith. This tendency toward nothingness might have been a source of unity between 19th century European nihilists against the apparent fatalism inherent in institutional religion, pg. 150.

Index

Godwin, William (b.1756-1836) – English writer and philosopher. Malthus' *An Essay on the Principle of Population* was a response to an essay by Godwin on avarice and profusion, pg. 89.

Gold Rush (1848) – President Polk and the beginning of a sovereign source of US currency bullion in California, pg. 216. | The Comstock lode in Nevada (1859): pg. 192.

H

Haavara Agreement (1933) – A relocation plan by the German NSDAP to help finance Jewish settlement in Palestine, pg. 237.

Habsburg – Austrian and last major Catholic monarchy located in Vienna that ruled over a considerable realm from 1282 to 1918, pg. 36.

Hayek, Freidrich (b.1899-1992) – Libertarian writer and Austrian theory economist. | Fascism: pg. 177, 228. | MMT: pg. 224.

Herzl, Theodor (b.1860-1904) – Lawyer, activist and writer; leader of the 19th century Zionist movement, pg. 32-36.

Hirsch, Baron Maurice de (b.1831-1896) – Financier and philanthropist who often helped relocate displaced European Jews, pg. 35.

Hitler, Adolph (b.1889-1945) – Leader of the German NSDAP party whose controversial biography *Mein Kampf* (1925) referred to years of "*Lies, Stupidity and Cowardice.*"; fascist whose contempt of the Jewish people, particularly in banking, might have paved the way for the establishment of the State of Israel, pg. 37, 237-238. (See also 'Haavara Agreement')

Index

I

Inflation – A distortion in the perception of value in an economic system, pg. 55, 129-130, 174, 210, 214-217. | Roman empire, pg. 182-183. | Fiat currency: pg. 190. | China: pg. 199-203. | The Great Depression: pg. 227. | The Federal Reserve: pg. 232, 249.

Inquisition, The – Catholic courts of inquiry that sought to counter apostasy and heresy primarily in Europe from the 12th to 15th centuries. | Ecclesiastical courts: pg. 149.

Intercession – Prayer through proxy; usually a saint or other Biblical figure, pg. 47, 119.

J

James VI (b.1566-1625) – King of Scotland, England and Ireland; patron of the most widely used Bible in the English language. | *Basilika Doron*: pg. 206.

Jung, Carl (b.1875-1861) – Swiss psychologist who disagreed with Freud about the formation of human character; known for his theory of a collective unconscious, pg. 158.

K

Keynes, John Maynard (b.1883-1946) – Highly influential English economist almost always associated with fiat monetary systems rather than the foreign exchange system after the Bretton Woods conference, pg. 177, 225, 227-230. | New Keynesian Theory: pg. 202.

Knapp, Georg Friedrich (b.1842-1926) – German academic, Chartelist and author of *The State Theory of Money*, pg. 223-227.

Index

Knights Templar – Christian group who might have created the first system of secure cross-border monetary transfer and exchange, pg. 147.

Kristallnacht – Riots across Germany against Jewish property on the 9th and 10th of November, 1938, pg. 237.

L

Lincoln, Abraham (b.1809-1865) – 16th President of the United States. | Labor: pg. 176. | Legal Tender and Banking Acts: pg. 214. | The Great Society: pg. 245.

Luther, Martin (b.1483-1546) – German priest and theologian whose disagreement with Roman Catholic doctrine started the Protestant movement, pg. 169.

M

Malthus, Thomas (b.1766-1834) – Church of England cleric and academic. | Morality: pg. 8. | *An Essay on the Principle of Population* (1798): pg. 89, 168. | Marriage: pg. 89, 91. | Virtue and perfection: pg. 89, 92. | Promiscuity in Shakespeare's *Antony and Cleopatra*: pg. 90-91. | Poor Laws: pg. 93. | Political Economy: pg. 165. | Ricardo: pg. 167-171. | Ireland: pg. 170-171.

Marx, Karl (b.1818-1883) – German philosopher who with Friedrich Engels wrote *The Communist Manifesto*; a mission statement of a new form of proletarian government. {Marxist} Economic theory generally implying State owned means of production and employment, pg. 174-176, 225, 243. | Labor and Capital: pg. 178. 181.

Index

Ming (dynasty) – Emperors of China 1368-1644, pg. 203-204.

Mises, Ludwig von (b.1881-1973) – Economist and member of the Austrian school. | Ayn Rand: pg. 159. | MMT: pg. 224. | Consumerism: pg. 228.

Money – Despite being a store of value and a means of exchange, this book is based on the idea that money and the monetary system are primarily based on faith, pg. 200. | Freedom: pg. 69. | Mammon and Mithras: pg. 135-136. | Materialism and the 'Root of evil': pg. 15-16, 140. | Pharisees: pg. 29, 76, 114-115.

N

Nero (b.37-68) – Roman emperor who preceded the Flavians and Rome's transition from pagan to Catholic, pg. 141, 182.

New Deal – American economic revitalization plan in the 1930s led by then President Roosevelt (FDR), pg. 94, 181, 239. | The Great Society: pg. 245.

Nostradamus (b.1503-1566) – French oracle who predicted world events well into the future, pg. 150.

Nixon, Richard M. (b.1913-1994) - 37th President of the United States. {Nixon Shock} The date when the Federal Reserve was ordered to stop making payments in gold, pg. 211, 245, 248.

O

Oppenheimer, J. Robert (b.1904-1967) – Liaison with the US Department of Defense during the Manhattan Project in Los Alamos, New Mexico; usually given credit for building the first atomic bomb (See also 'Fermi, Enrico'), pg. 150.

Index

P

Paley, William (b.1703-1805) – Anglican philosopher and theologian known for his Watchmaker theory, pg. 8-9, 21.

Paracelsus (b.1493-1541) – Swiss physician and philosopher whose work influenced the later Rosicrucian movement, pg. 152.

Peloponnesian War – Early fifth century BC Greek conflict, pg. 161.

Pilate, Pontius – First century Roman governor of Judea, pg. 6, 28-29.

Plato – Ancient Greek philosopher; writer of the dialogue *Republic* c.375 BC. | Democracy: pg. 162, 183.

Polk, James K. (b.1795-1849) – 11th US President whose sound monetary policies conflicted with the idea of a central bank, pg. 216.

Polo, Marco – Italian whose book *The Travels of Marco Polo* described China during the Yuan dynasty, pg. 200.

Proletarian – A secular bourgeois ambition that replaces religion with working-class labor, pg. 9, 37, 219. | Religion and faith, pg. 161-162, 167, 238. | Free-thought and liberty: pg. 59, 205-206. | Capitalism: pg. 73-74, 173, 210, 219-221. | Debt and credit: 232.

R

Rand, Ayn (b.1905-1982) – Russian-American writer, pg. 157-159.

Index

Rawls, John Bordley (b.1921-2002) – Harvard professor who formulated the idea of Original Position and Veiled Ignorance within the framework of liberal justice. | The Difference Principle and the Great Society, pg. 245-246.

Reformation – The 16th century, when the English monarchy separated from Catholic Rome, pg. 40. | Queen Mary and Elizabeth I: pg. 120-121, 125-126. | Dissolution of Monasteries: pg. 164.

Reich, Third – A book, *Das Dritter Reich* (1923) by German author Arthur Moeller van den Bruck criticized the Weimar Republic and heavily influenced members of a 1930s German political party – the NSDAP, with the idea that the Holy Roman Empire (800-1806) and the German Empire (1871-1918) would be succeeded by another thousand year Reich, pg. 238.

Religion (Institutional) - Anglican: pg. 8, 20, 89-90, 167-168, 171. | Catholic: pg. 20, 36, 48, 50, 56, 49, 120-128, 148-149, 164, 237. | Jewish: pg. 8, 12, 19, 47, 161-162. | Lutheran: pg. 169. | Orthodox: pg. 46-48, 50. | Protestant: pg. 50, 130, 171.

Ricardo, David (b.1772-1823) – Financier, member of Parliament and economist, pg. 8, 165, 167-171. (See also 'Malthus, Thomas')

Roosevelt, Franklin Delano (FDR) (b.1882-1945) – US President during the Great Depression, pg. 94, 177-181. (See also 'New Deal') | Executive Order 6102: pg. 211-212, 239. | Banking and Gold Reserve Act, 1934: pg. 239. | New World Order: pg. 241-242.

Rothschild, Baron Lionel Nathan de (b.1808-1879) – British banker, philanthropist, member of Parliament and the House of Lords whose family's considerable wealth helped finance the State of Israel. | Jewish Relief Act, 1858: pg. 19. | Balfour Declaration: pg. 234.

Index

S

Scrip – Paper issued by commercial interests with a third party guarantee, usually banknotes; particularly popular with shopkeepers and businesses in small towns before the US Civil War; a replacement for coins during shortages of metal, pg. 60.

Shakespeare, William (b.1564-1616) – English playwright. | *The Merchant of Venice*: pg. 16. | *Antony and Cleopatra*: pg. 89-90.

Smith, Adam (b.1723-1790) – Scottish economist; author of *An Inquiry into the Nature and Causes of the Wealth of Nations*; source of the idea that an 'invisible hand' regulates prices in a free market economy. | Coins and metal: pg. 69, 251. | 'Brain Drain': pg. 164. | Political Economy: pg. 165. | Ricardo: pg. 169. | Colonial America: pg. 207-209. | Stock and credit: pg. 230.

Stater – Coin of the Lydian empire, pg. 100.

T

Trinity – {1} An ecclesiastical term derived from the blood, water and Spirit in 1 John 5:5-8 (See also 'Agape'), pg. 51, 106, 111, 137. {2} A Catholic doctrine of the Father, Son and Holy Spirit. {3} The Manhattan Project and a name given to the first atomic bomb test in 1945: pg. 148.

W

Webster, Daniel (b.1782-1852) – Legendary American politician fictionalized by writer Stephen Vincent Benét in the book *The Devil and Daniel Webster* (1936). Story implies that it would take a lawyer with an exceptional talent to cancel the obligation of a sinful contract, pg. 61.

Index

Whately, Richard (b.1787-1863) – Church of England Archbishop and prolific writer on many subjects including the economy. | *Lessons on Morals* and Paley's Watchmaker theory: pg. 8-13, 21. | Aristotle's *Ethics*: pg. 10. | Matthew 7:12: pg. 13. | *Christian Evidences*: pg. 106. | *Easy Lessons on Money Matters*: pg. 129-133.

Y

Yuan – {dynasty} The emperors of China from 1271 to 1368, after the Song and before the Ming, ruled by Mongol emperor Kublai Khan. {currency} A unit of exchange in present day China. | Fiat currency: pg. 200-204.

Z

Zion – The hill where Jerusalem originally stood; by extension refers to the Israel of scripture as well as contested land in Palestine. {Zionism} A 19th century revival of Jewish cultural identity that included a return to a homeland in the Middle East by Jews scattered all over the world after the diaspora. (See also 'Balfour Declaration') {Zionist} An individual, particularly a gentile, who believes in the authority of the law, primarily the law of the Jews, pg. 15-17, 21, 33, 31-35. (See also 'Herzl, Theodor') | Fascism: pg. 6, 145, 177, 181.

Acknowledgments

Book jacket, bookplate, images on pages 28, 33, 38, 68, 80, 86, 96, 113, 118, 120, 144, 156, 236, 240 and text quoted within chapter Conclusion are the product of Artificial Intelligence (Ai).

"The People vs. the Crown" on page 38 and "A Self-Determined Nation" on page 42 contain information from Wikipedia.org.

"Timeline of that 'Other' Metal" on page 174 contains information from www.gainesvillecoins.com.

a Selected Bibliography

of rare & out-of-print books

Garrett, Garet - *The Devil's Bushel*, E.P. Dutton & Co., 1924.

Herzl, Theodor - *A Jewish State*, 1896. English translation by Sylvie d'Avigdor.

Herzl, Theodor - *The Congress Addresses of Theodor Herzl*, 1917. English translation by Nellie Straus.

Herzl, Theodor - *The Complete Diaries of Theodor Herzl, Vol. 1*, Patai & Zohn, 1960.

Keynes, John M. - *A Tract on Monetary Reform*, Macmillan & Co., 1923.

Knapp, Georg F. - *The State Theory of Money*, 4th ed., 1923. English translation by Lucas & Sanger.

Malthus, Thomas R. - *An Essay on the Principle of Population*, 6th ed., John Murray publisher, 1798.

Marx, Karl - *Wage, Labour and Capital*, 1849. English translation by Unknown.

a Selected Bibliography

Rand, Ayn - *Anthem*, Cassell and Company, 1938.

Ricardo, David - *On the Principles of Political Economy, and Taxation*, John Murray publisher, 1817.

Ricardo, David - *Proposals for an Economical and Secure Currency*, 3rd ed., John Murray publisher, 1819.

Ricardo, David - *The Letters of David Ricardo to Thomas Malthus*. James Bonar editor, 2011.

Say, J. B. - *Letters to Mr. Malthus ... to Which is Added A Catechism of Political Economy*, Sherwood, Neely and Jones publisher, 1821. English translation by John Richter.

Whately, Richard - *Easy Lessons on Money Matters*, 13th ed., John W. Parker publisher, 1853.

Whately, Richard - *Peculiarlarities of the Christian Religion*, 7th ed., John W. Parker publisher, 1856.

Whately, Richard - *Lessons on Morals and Christian Evidences*, John Bartlett publisher, 1857.

Whately, Richard - *Paley's Moral Philosophy*, John W. Parker publisher, 1859.